Other books by George Emanuels

YGNACIO VALLEY 1834-1970

WALNUT CREEK—ARROYO DE LAS NUECES

JOHN MUIR INVENTOR

CALIFORNIA'S CONTRA COSTA COUNTY—
AN ILLUSTRATED HISTORY

OUR FIRST ONE HUNDRED YEARS

CALIFORNIA INDIANS

AN

ILLUSTRATED

GUIDE

By

GEORGE EMANUELS

WALNUT CREEK, CALIFORNIA 1990

First edition

ISBN 3-9607520-3-X

Published and distributed by
George Emanuels dba DIABLO BOOKS
1317 Canyonwood #1
Walnut Creek, California 94595
Telephone (415) 939-8644

CONTENTS

ACKNOWLEDGEMENTS

The author wants his readers to know the sources of the material he used in preparing this book. He has done no original research himself. Rather, all of the material used in the work is that of a number of recognized ethnologists and their students, beginning with that journalist and keen observer, Stephen Powers (1840-1918), who wrote the first formal ethnographical survey of California Indians in 1877.

Ethnologists whose works have been gleaned include: C. Hart Merriam (1855-1942), Alfred L. Kroeber (1876-1960), and Robert F. Heizer (1915-1979).

The Lowie Museum of Anthropology on the Berkeley campus of the University of California supplied almost a quarter of the illustrations used. San Francisco photographer Todd Pickering made many more copies from published works.

The University of California Press, Berkeley, has been very cooperative and generous by allowing the use of many pictures in their publications.

My son, Roger Emanuels, has edited when given the opportunity and contributed his expertise in many ways. My wife, Helen, is my faithful proofreader.

Daniel Hersh, the Reference Librarian at Contra Costa County's Main Library, went out of his way to assist me in procuring dozens of the illustrations I've used. A special "Thanks" to him.

I owe the idea and encouragement for a book on California Indians for people of all ages whose interest in the subject would be increased by the use of numerous illustrations, to a valued friend, Robert L. Hawley, one of California's premier scarce and rare book dealers of Albany, California.

The Author

INTRODUCTION

To begin to understand the native Californians one has only to read Don Gaspar Portolá's account of meeting them. No other explorer came overland before Portolá so his record gives a very true picture of the California Indian before his contact with Europeans.

Following is the translation of what he saw and experienced along the Indian trail north from San Diego. He set out from his base camp at San Diego Bay on July 14, 1769 and measured his distances in Spanish leagues, a distance of approximately 3 miles each.

From San Diego — 26 leagues. "The Indians of a village...came over unarmed, with unmatched friendliness and peacefulness, made us a present of their poor seeds and were treated by us."

From San Diego — 33 leagues. "A populous village of Indians who received us with great friendliness. Fifty two of their number came over to our camp, and their chief or headman told us with much pleading...that we should stay and live with them, (that) they would provide us our sustenance."

From San Diego 48 leagues. "We found a village of heathens, very friendly; at once they visited our quarters with bowls of seed foods, nuts and acorns."

From San Diego — 58 leagues. "A crowd of Indians came over to the camp with a present of seeds, acorns and canegrass honeycomb, a very friendly affectionate folk."

From San Diego — 64 leagues. "Seven chiefs came over with a bountiful present of seeds, acorns, nuts, and pine nuts which they spread before us."

From San Diego — 73 leagues. "We placed our camp next to a temporary village of Indian fishermen who made us a present of more fish than we could eat."

As he continued on Portolá experienced similar help all along the way until his men halted at the barrier in their path, the Golden Gate. Then and only then, did natives show him any hostility.

Without an armed conflict the expedition turned about and headed back to San Diego. From approximately San Luis Obispo south his record states, "The Indians of this town presented us with quantities of fresh and dried fish, a great deal of sardines and bonitos, so that we began, thank God, to see plenty prevail in our camp."

Five years later Fray Pedro Font, the spiritual leader of Anza's California Colony, came north in Portolá's footsteps. While in the Santa Barbara area Font observes, "Yet I saw very few women close at hand, for as soon as they saw us they all hastily hid in their huts, especially the girls, the men remaining outside blocking the doors and taking care that nobody should go inside...This is the result of the outrages and extortions which the soldiers have perpetrated when in their journeys they have passed along the Channel, especially in the beginning."

Thus the Europeans betrayed the goodwill shown them. Nevertheless, for at least the next fifty years, the natives both north and south, upon meeting the white man for the first time, extended the hand of friendship.

Where did they all go? What happened to them? For obvious reasons no count of the natives was ever made but estimates have been made that as many as 360,000 natives lived in California in the very early 1800s.

By 1900 probably no more than 15,000 Indians remained.

The men from San Diego to Sonoma and from the coast up into the gold region were made slaves. Every large landowner but John Bidwell, who came to Butte County in 1841, had his slave quarters. Slaves kept away from their women don't father children, hence the birth rate dropped sharply after the European arrival.

Even small ranchers had their captives. One Granville Swift, an illiterate miner, made a fortune by making his natives bring him the results of their digging. When they brought him less than he wanted he whipped them and confined them at night. When he built his stone house, Temelec Hall, in Sonoma in 1858, he again used Indian slaves as workers. When he worked them by day he chained their ankles to cannon balls, and at night chained them to the walls of their barracks.

Indians succumbed to smallpox in large numbers. Epidemics broke out all over California. In 1838, one surfaced to the north of San Francisco Bay within the confines of General Vallejo's jurisdiction, where deaths among the natives were estimated at 60,000 to 75,000.

Earlier, in 1828-29, a smallpox epidemic ravaged the mission Indians all through the 21 missions.

Any estimate of those natives who died from gunshot wounds would have to be placed at least at 100,000. Mexican soldiers ambushed them and when the State joined the Union the United States Army continued the slaughter. On one foray alone in Sonoma County, Salvador Vallejo, brother of the General, led his Mexican troops and his Indian allies, the Suisuns, north pursuing the Sotoyomi tribe. One Sotoyomi had stolen one the General's mules. The tribe seized Vallejo's envoy who had been sent to return the animal and tortured the man. In revenge the expedition killed 800 Indians and took 300 more prisoner. Certainly the prisoners became Vallejo's slaves.

When settlers moved into Mendocino, Humboldt and Del Norte Counties in the 1850s they began destroying some of the Indian's way of life. The U. S. Army went in to keep peace between the natives and the whites which resulted in more Indian bloodletting. Indians took revenge on the settlers and the settlers did the same on the natives. Every Indian became fair game for any miner or farmer who looked down the sights of his rifle and saw a native within range. No estimate has been made of the number killed but the troops were not withdrawn until 1865. In the winter of 1858-59 ninety troops killed an estimated ninety Indians, and not all were males. In another action in February 1860 nearly 300 Indians died and at least half were women and children.

This book describes "tribes" as family groups who shared a common language. They were not groups who lived and worked together. Each family group generally kept its independence, except when need required a larger group of people.

Almost fifty years after Fray Serra established the first mission at San Diego, a ship's doctor wrote his impressions of the California natives. The Italian, Paolo Emilio Botta in 1827 made these observations: "The men are of medium height, their skin a deep bronze color, their hands so small sometimes they don't fit in with the rest of their body. Their narrow foreheads and puffed out cheeks…they have little eyes which are always black…their nose is generally flat, wide at the base. The mouth is large and is usually adorned with very white and very straight teeth…they seldom have beards…(at the missions) nearly all speak Spanish. The Spaniards hate them…and mistreat them whenever they are able to do so."

The Italian's ship had touched at San Francisco (called Yerba Buena), Mission Santa Cruz, Monterey, Santa Barbara Mission, San Pedro (Mission San Gabriel), and San Diego.

"It is now about fifty years since the Spaniards have established themselves in that land, and have settled the Indians in their missions;…from that time on the depopulation has progressed…in the greater part of California…is at the present time almost deserted. [1827?] I heard from one of the missionaries that in his mission sixty marriages produced only eight children and of them only one survives now. Within twenty years if things continue…there will be only whites in California."

Horace Bell, a "ranger" in Southern California during the 1850s, 60s and 70s, published his views of the California Indians. Although he was noted for exaggeration, they reflected attitudes prevalent at the time.

"We will let those rascally redskins know they have no longer to deal with the Spaniards or the Mexicans, but with the invincible race of American backwoodsmen which has driven the savage from Plymouth Rock to the Rocky Mountains, and has headed him here on the western shore of the continent, and will drive him back to meet his kindred fleeing westward, all to be drowned in the Great Salt Lake."

It is two hundred years since our kind began elbowing our way in, moving the natives out, onto the margins of society, changing the land to suit ourselves, and polluting the air and water of California. The Indians lived here for thousands of years, living in peace, despoiling nothing, not knowing our greed, our hurry, or our reckless disregard for what others want.

It is good we see how these natives succeeded so well before we came.

Lowie Museum, Berkeley, California

This Yuki man's dance costume includes a flicker quill head band, head net filled with eagle down and forked feather plumes, a netted feather cape, and a deerskin shirt. Yuki specified a time of year when they confined all their young men in their dance house. During this period the tribal elders taught them tribal mythology and medical cures, such as curing rattlesnake bites and cases of poisoning. This man is dressed to impersonate a god or spirit.

TRIBAL AREAS
OF
CALIFORNIA

courtesy Pacific Western Traders, Folsom, Calif.

YUROK

Of all the tribes in California one tribe, small in numbers, who inhabited some of the northwest coast, maintained considerably more unusual practices than any other. Ethnologist Alfred Kroeber estimated their aboriginal population to have reached only 2,500 persons. They had no influence pressed on them by European explorers by sea, or by Spanish missionaries by land. The mountains of Del Norte County kept opportunists at bay and allowed members of the Yurok tribe uninterrupted years to develop their uniqueness.

They inhabited approximately a forty mile stretch of coastline, north and south from the mouth of the Klamath River. They also built their villages up that river to its junction with the Trinity. Along the stream they constructed their dwellings on the north bank so as to have the maximum sunlight available.

Their houses were one of the differences which set them apart from other California Indians. In setting them up they first excavated a round pit, four to five feet deep and twelve to fifteen feet in diameter. Over this excavation, instead of a domed thatched hut or the cone-shaped slab tepee so prevalent elsewhere, the Yurok built a square cabin as large as fifty feet on each side. They made the dwelling six to ten feet wider than the pit so as to have a wide shelf for storage and personal belongings within it.

The natives kept their fire going in the center of the pit and slept in a circle around it.

One of the most unusual features of the cabin was the design of

1

its entrance. Its function was to keep in as much heat and keep out the cold while persons went in and out. They made it out of a slab about three feet wide. Using flints for scrapers and elk horns for drills, they would cut out a hole in the slab just large enough for a person on all fours to crawl through. The low placement of the entrance insured a minimum of heat would escape the dwelling.

Another unique feature of the Yurok was their canoe production. Among their closest neighbors, the Karok and the Hupa, they alone with their coastal neighbors, the Tolowa, had an unending supply of redwood, both standing trees and logs washed up on their beaches. The Hupa and the Karok had no such supply and consequently purchased theirs from the Yurok. After white men arrived they would pay from $10 to $30 and more for a single boat.

Before iron tools reached the northwest it took the natives five to six months to burn out and scrape a log into a seaworthy vessel. In constructing their ocean-going canoes they burned them out of logs thirty to forty feet long and from five to ten feet in diameter. In these canoes they could easily carry a ton of fish. To light a fire exactly where they wanted it the men spread pitch over the spot. After they lit the fire, thus hollowing the place, they would put out the flame by slapping a piece of raw bark over it. Neither end of a Yurok dugout was pointed but instead was left blunt, the same width as the log it came from. At the stern, they would burn out a seat for the pilot, the most important man when navigating the boat through the ocean surf.

In one other aspect the Yurok achieved singular ability among California Indians. They built ocean-going canoes, dugouts to carry on a trade with their neighbors, as far as twenty-two miles, from the mouth of the Klamath, north against current and the usually brisk northwest winds. Just going through the surf at the mouth of the Klamath with a load of as much as a ton of salmon required a skill unknown elsewhere on the California coast.

One might compare them with the Chumash in their sewn-plank canoes, paddling across the Santa Barbara Channel. Seldom if ever were the Chumash canoes so heavily laden. Most often their prevailing wind and current were much more favorable than at Point St. George, five hundred miles north.

Lowie Museum, Berkeley, Calif.

Yurok fishermen on California's northwest coast caught their surf fish with a dip net. Ocean catches required a large net; in small streams they used the same shaped net but used a smaller size. They made their dip nets by bending a branch into a semicircular shaped frame, bisected by a handle.

They preserved most of their catch for future eating by sun drying the fish.

These Yurok are drying their fish on the shore of Redwood Lagoon, only a short walk from the ocean beach.

3

On their return trip after trading with the Wiyot to the south as far as present day Trinidad, and with the Tolowa to the north as far as Crescent City, they brought back articles not found in their area, and after 1850, the white man's manufactured goods.

Another unusual event keeps the Yurok in mind for another of his differences. Late in their culture, early in the 1900s, before 1910 when Alfred Kroeber estimated there were only 688 Yurok survivors, Yurok males became enfranchised. This was twenty years before California Indians elsewhere received the privilege to vote.

The aboriginal Yurok was dark complected, with those living near the ocean beaches being almost black. They were known for their low foreheads and a more than usual projecting chin. Early observers coming among them reported their speech to be unusually guttural.

With their neighbors up the Klamath and along the ocean they used the same hunting, fishing, and woodworking tools. They made fish nets of vines and netsinkers of stone. They used antlers for wedges to split wood, and stone hammers to drive the wedges. They used bone needles for weaving tule reeds into mats.

Their first contact with Europeans was brief. Hudson Bay Company trappers came through some Yurok villages in 1827 but didn't repeat beyond that first visit. The trappers did report they saw some American trade goods among the natives. The source of these foreign objects is unknown but are thought to have come from the

Lowie Museum, Berkeley, Calif.
The Yurok made these ornaments which they attached to the bow of their canoes.

YUROK

The Yurok made excellent canoes of a unique design. Their dugout, so shallow it had virtually no gunwale or freeboard, ideal for riding surf breakers and choppy waves included a carved wooden ornament affixed separately to the bow of the canoe.

When it came time to hunt sea lions the hunters needed to be prepared to go to sea for hours. They started by taking station on rocks, disguised in bear or deer skins. When the lions clambered up, the hunters barked and twisted their bodies, attracting the sea lions' attention as they approached, then leaped up and speared them.

They made no attempt to hold their prey, but they followed it in a canoe, and at the first opportunity they speared it again. Sometimes a canoe was dragged out to sea for half a day before they could kill it. For this reason large males were seldom attacked in late afternoon.

The Yurok carried on a trade with their upstream neighbors. The Karok preferred to buy their canoes from the Yurok rather than make them themselves.

wreck of a Yankee trading vessel.

In 1828 Jedediah Smith led his party of trappers through Yurok territory. He is known to have brought such trade goods with him as beads, knives, and iron arrow points.

A dual class system existed among the Yurok at least until the coming of the whites. An aristocracy, about ten percent of the males, defined by their wealth, owned heirlooms, and perpetuated itself by paying particular attention to its male children. They began a boy's education at age six. He learned to make a bow of yew, arrows of cedar, and a bow string of sinew. By age eight he knew the basis of his tribe's laws and some case precedents. He learned the value of listening, to comprehend what he heard.

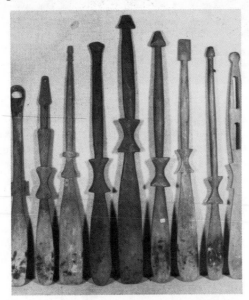

Lowie Museum, Berkeley, California

These paddles were used by both the Yuroks and the Hupas. Carving the grip for the left hand (for a right handed user) gives the paddler a non-slip hold, a help where hands or paddles were often wet and slippery. Although they had little contact with the white man and none with any missions, the Yurok population dropped from about 2,700 in 1870 to about 500-600 in 1910.

6

At age sixteen he went on a survival test in high mountains, staying long enough to experience a vision.

Only the richest men of the tribe owned slaves and then not more than two at a time. Some rich men ruled a small village, though not as its owner but rather because his wealth made him obviously superior.

One way a Yurok commoner had of keeping his children in line was with the implied threat in the demanding question, "Do you want to become a slave?"

Edward Curtis

This is the entrance to a Yurok sweathouse. It is so low as to allow little heat to escape the building. Each man to enter (women were not allowed), brought in with him a few sticks to burn and so kept the fire blazing. To provide extra insulation and thus keep in the maximum amount of heat, many sweathouses had earth covered roofs.

Often the floor was below the surrounding earth level, usually dug out to two or three feet.

The coastal Yurok bathed regularly as if to start the day more fully awake. He would groggily crawl from his hut and run into the ocean. Briskly rubbing himself in salt water he would step ashore and shake himself off.

Yurok law specified compensation for an insult, a death or an injury, and even for destruction of property. To settle disputes, a negotiator or go-between made the decision as to the amount of compensation.

While intermarriage took place early in the 1850s, many native customs remained in place for several decades. In 1851, each aristocrat's grave was fenced and the top of each picket was decorated with feathers. Graves were decorated with baskets, with the bottoms broken out and laid upside down. Traditionally, a widower or widow sat around his or her deceased partner's grave for several nights to give the soul a chance to go wherever souls went.

J. Goldsborough Bruff described in his journal, *Gold Rush*, the death of a young chief and the attention his spouse gave him.

"The grave of a chief. With feathers around pallisade & son kill'd by the Indians at Forks of Trinity & Klamath—the (Eurocks) 100 mi. distant, and mountainous wooded road; from whence his squaw packed him down on her back in 2 1/2 days. Young chief named Largo—son of the Morweme (chief).

"In Feby 1850—when Largo's wife brought in his remains, the Indians inform'd the whites at Trinidad & invited them to attend the funeral. His squaw prepared the body for interment by washing & marking over it, many stripes of black—put his beads, wampum &c. in his hands, envellop'd the body in skins; laid mats in the bottom of the grave, after digging it herself, and assisted by the whites, laid the body on back, placing shells, &c &c—on breast—cov'd it up. Women howling around, & old chief (the father) standing on sweathouse directing."

The Yurok, though not the finest marksman in all of California, did excel. Charles Wilkes, Commander of the United States Exploring Expedition in 1841, saw bowmen who could hit a button three times out of five, at sixty feet.

Loeffelholz, a German gold miner at Trinidad Bay, saw a Yurok "strike a 10¢ piece, at a distance of twenty paces, six time out of 10."

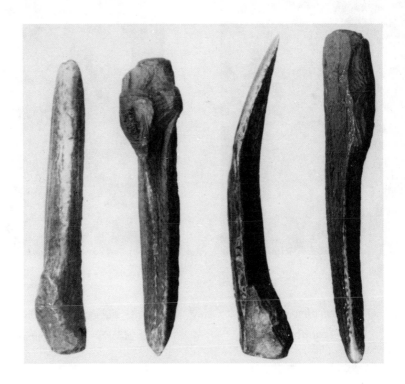

Lowie Museum, Berkeley, Calif.

The Yurok split redwood logs driving wedges made of elk horns. They dressed them with the same tools.

They built their houses from 18 to 25 square feet, always around a square or rectangular pit.

The men wore no regular clothing, using skins when the weather required, while the women wore skirts of dressed skins or sometimes of bark and cloaks of fur in the cold season.

Unusual for California Indians, the Yurok had no chiefs to lead them. Prominence among them depended on wealth.

Edward Curtis

Edward Curtis

*This is a view of a Yurok
cemetery about 1910.*

*Note the basket hat on
this elderly Yurok woman.*

KAROK

"The Karok are the finest race in all that region", so reported journalist Stephen Powers in 1877. By "all that region", Powers was probably referring to the area from Mt. Shasta, down the Klamath River, to its junction with the Trinity River, and very likely all of Trinity County.

From where the Klamath met the Trinity, upstream for more than forty miles, over one hundred villages lay along the banks of the Klamath.

The most important Karok food supply came from three sources: the river and its plentiful supply of fish, the groves of oak trees from which they gathered and stored acorns, and lastly from the forests that covered the mountains where they hunted mainly deer.

Fortunately the Karok lived without contact with the Missions and missionaries, thus living their traditional lives for three-quarters of a century longer than the natives around San Francisco Bay. They maintained their way of life until interrupted by the miners who came in numbers to some of their villages in 1850.

Unique to the Karok was the respect and high social position they accorded those who accumulated property. The person to whom they gave unusual respect was the one who had stored up the most woodpecker scalps, obsidian blades or shell money. They esteemed a thrifty person and one who was moderate in eating and drinking habits. They believed one way to riches was to stay busy and work hard. Mothers, whenever possible, taught their children to look down on lazy people.

Like many California tribes the Karok recognized no tribal

chieftain. Rather, the rich men of a village led their many families much as wealthy citizens today lead and influence our civic governments. Too, each family expected its wealthy elders to maintain harmony by educating its young, and to discipline its own members as needed.

A young suitor sought the approval of the girl's parents by bartering and negotiating with them. His success as a hunter or his ability had nothing to do with the parents making their decision. His ability to pay decided whether or not he got the girl. From the parents' standpoint, the more the young man paid, the higher their status in the village. Strangely enough, the more the young man had to pay, the

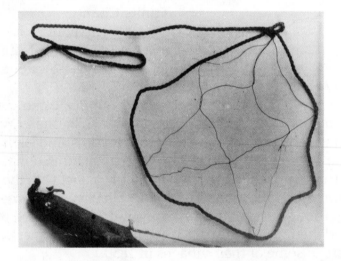

Lowie Museum, Berkeley, Calif.
This snare is the kind the Karok used to catch deer. When hunting they would lie in wait near a salt lick or near a spring. So that their human odors would not reveal their presence they would often smear their bodies with yerba buena (good herb). They would lie in ambush in thick brush along the trail and wait for a deer to step into their snare and then quickly tighten it around the animal's leg.

KAROK

Klamath River lodge and sweathouse.

Stephen Powers, 1877, Univ. of California Press

greater airs he could display among his friends. In 1877, Stephen Powers described the Karok motivation to require the suitor to pay them well, because, "that family is most aristocratic, in which the most money is paid for the wife".

Man and wife didn't sleep together in Karok life. Virtually all women slept indoors with their children while men slept in the warm sweathouse. On reaching three years of age, the boys left their mothers' arms and went to spent the nights with their fathers. For many hours the boys listened to their fathers, giving the men their undivided attention. Boys repeatedly heard admonitions, learned the taboos, and listened to their fathers' accomplishments, feats and experiences. They heard how to survive in war and in the hunt.

While storytelling often contained moral lessons, it also resulted in passing along myths and traditions. A child received most of his or her education by listening to a parent or grandparent storyteller.

Myths often told how the world was made and how birds, fish, animal, and humans were created. Journalist Stephen Powers published several Karok myths in 1877, one of which tells of the creation of salmon.

"When Kareya (who created the world) made all things which have breath, he first made the fishes in the big water, then the animals, and last of all The Man. But Kareya did not let the fishes come up the Klamath, and thus the Karok had not enough food, and were sore ahungered. There were salmon in the big water, many and very fine to eat, but no Indian could catch them in the big water; and Kareya had made a great fish dam at the mouth of the Klamath and closed it fast, and given the key to two old hags to keep, so that the salmon could not go up the river. And the hags kept the key that Kareya had given them, and watched it day and night without sleeping, so that no Indian could come near it.

"Then the Karok were sore disturbed in those days

for the lack of food, and many died, and their children cried to them because they had no meat. But the coyote befriended the Karok, and helped them, and took it upon himself to bring the salmon up the Klamath. First he went to an alder tree and gnawed off a piece of bark, for the bark of the alder tree after it is taken off presently turns red and looks like salmon. He took the piece of alder bark in his teeth and journeyed far down the Klamath until it came to the mouth of it at the big water. Then he rapped at the door of the cabin where the old hags lived and when they opened it he said "*Ai-yu-kwai*", for he was very polite. And they did not wonder to hear the coyote speak in those days. They did

This Karok man represents what the student ethnologist Stephen Powers described in 1877 as "probably the finest tribe in California. Their stature is only a trifle under the American; they have well-sized bodies, erect and strongly knit together, and when a Karok has a weapon to which he is accustomed, a sharp stone gripped in the hand, he will face a white man and give him a handsome fight." Both Karok men and women made a daily habit of bathing in the cold water of the nearest stream.

not suspect the coyote, and so asked him to come into their cabin and sit by the fire. This he did, and after he warmed himself a while he commenced nibbling his piece of alder bark. One of the hags seeing this said to the other, "See, he has some salmon!" So they were deceived and thrown off their guard and presently one of them rose, took down the key and went to get some salmon to cook for themselves. Thus the coyote saw where the key was kept, but he was not much better off than before for it was too high for him to reach it. The hags cooked some salmon for supper and ate it, but they gave the coyote none.

"So he stayed in the cabin all night with the hags pretending to sleep, but he was thinking how to get the key and started to get some salmon again, and the coyote happened to think of a way as quick as a flash. He jumped up and darted under the hag, which threw her down, and caused her to fling the key a long way off. The coyote quickly seized it in his teeth and ran and opened the fish dam before the hags could catch him. Then the salmon were allowed to go up the Klamath, and the Karok had plenty of food."

Edward Curtis

This Indian is paddling his balsa, square-ended canoe carrying a basket for trapping fish. He is probably a Modoc. This tribe is noted for its almost infinite use of bulrush. From it they made mats, house coverings, rafts, quivers, moccasins, leggings, eye shields and baby cradles.

Unlike most California Indians who either cremated their dead or buried them in the fetal position, the Karok buried theirs with the body stretched out. Beside the body relatives placed all the departed one's ordinary clothing all of which they then buried with the deceased. His wealth, which included his best clothing and personal property, was kept out in order to display them, for as long as they survived the elements, on top of the pickets of a fence built to enclose the grave. If the deceased was a woman, her best baskets were hung from the pickets of her fence.

The grave was generally dug by male relatives close to the cabin of the deceased. It was their duty to sleep alongside the grave for five consecutive nights. Five nights were believed long enough to ensure the soul enough time to reach that land of happiness in the sky.

In memory of her dead husband, a widow would cut her hair close to the scalp, and keep it short until she remarried.

The Karok sincerely revered the memory of their dead. One of the most serious offenses a person could commit was to speak the dead relative's name. So serious a violation was it that atonement could only be made by paying blood money, an amount equal to that paid by a murderer. They did not like strangers to even inspect a relative's gravesite.

The Karok believed the deceased could hear them if, before burial, they spoke into the dead person's ear. Stephen Powers witnessed such a scene and described it in *Tribes of California*:

"One of his children died, and he had decently prepared it for burial, carried it in his own arms and laid it in its lonely grave on the steep mountainside, amid the green and golden ferns, where the spiry pines mournfully soughed in the wind, chanting in their sad threnody [song of lamentation], while the swamp-stained Klamath roared over the rocks far, far below. He was about to cast the first shovelful of earth down upon it, when an Indian woman, a near relative of the child, descended into the grave, bitterly weeping, knelt down beside the little one, and amid that shuddering and broken sobbing which only women know in their passionate sorrow, murmured in its ear:

17

"O, darling, my dear one, goodbye! Nevermore shall your little hands softly clasp these old withered cheeks, and your pretty feet shall print the moist earth around my cabin nevermore. You are going on a long journey to the spirit-land, and you must go alone, for none of us can go with you. Listen, then, to the words I speak to you and heed them well, for I speak the truth. In the spirit-land there are two roads. One of them is a path of roses, and it leads to the Happy Western Land beyond the great water, where you shall see your dear mother. The other is a path strewn with thorns and briers, and leads, I know not whither, to an evil and dark land, full of deadly serpents, where you would wander forever. O, dear child, choose you the path of roses, which leads to the Happy Western Land, a fair and sunny land, beautiful as the morning. And may the great Kareya help you to walk in it to the end, for your little tender feet must walk alone. O, darling, my dear one, good-bye!"

Lowie Museum, Berkeley, Calif.

This Karok fisherman is using another version of the dip net. He sets his on the bottom and awaits a salmon to run into it.

As placer mining yielded less and less gold along the creeks of the Mother Lode in the Sierra foothills, prospectors came north in search of the easily found deposits so abundant in 1848 and 1849. By 1850 they had disrupted the Karok way of life, muddying the Klamath tributaries, and setting up camp wherever they wished without regard for the natives. Violence broke out as the Indians resisted the trespassers while the gun-toting whites pressed their way in.

Among the many killings which resulted, the following letter illustrates the condition facing the Karok. in 1852.

Lowie Museum, Berkeley, Calif.
This Karok Indian is fishing for salmon in the Klamath River with a triangular shaped framed net. The natives dried most of their catch during the salmon runs and hung it from the rafters of their huts. They tried to store enough fish to last until the next year's run.

Alta California, **May 21, 1852**

Your correspondent also labors under a mistake in representing the late killing of some 40 Indians at the Upper Crossing as occurring in a 'fight'. It was cold-blooded, unprovoked massacre. An Indian, sometime in the early part of March, had been shot by a white man at Happy Camp. The Indians on the rivers above were exasperated, and perhaps threatened retaliation. At all events, some miners were alarmed, raised a party, surrounded the Rancheria at the Ferry, and killed every man and some women; then proceeding up the river 2 miles, surrounded another village and killed every man but one, who escaped wounded, making a total of some 30 or 40 killed. All accounts agree in stating that the attack was wholly unlooked for by the Indians, who from the date of the treaty at Scott's Valley in November, had been perfectly quiet and inoffensive. The facts are given on the authority of the Special Indian Agent in that neighborhood, who investigated the sad affair in connection with Capt. Charles McDermit and Mr. Owens, who resides in the immediate vicinity. It is quite too common for letter writers and editors in California to represent every difficulty which occurs on the frontier, as an aggression or outrage on the part of the Indians, and in justifying the most severe punishment, even their downright butchery. Like all wild, untutored nations, they may be revengeful and treacherous; but it is a most remarkable fact that all the tribes with whom treaties have been made by the United States Agents during the past year, have so far, most religiously observed their engagements. No single case of murder or other outrage upon the whites can be traced to any of these tribes. Where difficulties have existed, the whites have been the aggressors, or the Indians were of the tribes not yet visited by the Agents. This statement may be denied, but it cannot be disproved. I wish for the credit of the whites that the facts were different.

Very Respectfully,
R. McKee

In the 1840s, before the white miners and settlers invaded their territory, it has been estimated that 2,700 Karoks were living in the more than 100 villages.

About 1851, military operations, executions by the settlers, and venereal disease brought to them by the whites, had reduced their numbers to only about 1,050 persons.

That number grew for about 15 years and then started dropping off again. By 1910 the number of full-blooded Karoks remaining was estimated to be between only 700-800 persons.

Today, in 1990, Karok descendants continue to create traditional costumes, do the traditional dances, and otherwise maintain traditional Karok spirituality.

Lowie Museum, Berkeley, Calif.

This Karok fisherman is using a plunge net in rough water on the Klamath River. In essence he will dip the net, and then scoop up the fish he is after. During the few weeks of the annual salmon run a Karok will expect to catch enough fish which he will dry, to last his family until the following year's run. He will dry the fish first on a scaffold out in the open and later hang them from the roof supports in his dwelling.

KAROK

Viola Roseberry

Karok women living along the five mile stretch of the junction of the Klamath and the Salmon Rivers made these baskets. They used hazel twigs, strands from the roots of sugar pine, and sometimes strands of spruce roots. For black they wove a special maidenhair fern; for red they used alder-dyed fibres or a large woodwardie fern; for white, squaw grass (tanax). The design of the large plate on top represents running water from a spring on the mountain side. The old war apron belonged to Chief White Devil. The picture was made in 1915.

HUPA

Where the north end of the Sacramento Valley runs into the forested mountains, today one can turn west and drive along steep canyons, over bridges and reach the homeland of the Hupa Indians. No road went into the forests before 1850 and invading miners stayed out of the Hupa's territory until they had muddied most gold bearing streams in Northern California.

Deep in the wilderness, far from the Sacramento Valley a mighty river cut its way west. The Trinity River grew as it drained the thousands of creeks along its path until it met the Klamath and there surrendered its water.

The Hoopa Valley includes the junction of the two rivers and here the natives who called themselves "Nalinook-wa" lived. Their coastal neighbors to the northwest, the Yurok, replaced the four syllable word with one only half as long, "Hoopah", now shortened to "Hupa".

From Hoopa Valley upstream for about sixty miles along the Trinity, the Hupa populated twelve principal villages. They built their houses of cedar slabs set on end, the walls usually four feet high on the sides and six feet high at the ends, thus allowing for the roof slope. They made a hole about 20 inches in diameter for their entrance, starting it about a foot off the ground.

They started building a house by digging a five foot deep hole, twelve feet square and lined its walls with stone. Over the twelve foot square excavation they built their 20 foot square slab structure thus allowing four feet of "shelf" all the way around the interior on which to store firewood and personal belongings. A plank stairway led from the upper level to the lower.

Honored guests and men of the tribe sat across from the entrance, women and children on either side of them, and those of lesser importance, on space closest to the entrance.

The fire in the sunken section served as a cooking fire but also kept the house warm throughout the night, so well did the cedar slabs insulate it from the cold.

The women and children slept in the house but the men spent the nights in their sweathouse where upon awakening, warm and sometimes perspiring, they would eagerly go out and plunge into the close by stream.

Edward Curtis
No fire burned at night in this Hupa sweathouse, but so tightly was it built, after the men sleeping there at night would wake up perspiring, they would go out and plunge into the river.

Except for the powerful Karok to the northeast and the Yurok to the west the Hupa held all six of their neighboring tribes as vassals. They kept them under a heavy hand, under submission, exacting tribute in return for peace. The tribute usually took the form of animal skins or shell money and they required the six tribes to speak their language.

Stephen Powers, Univ. of California Press

A student of Indian ethnology, Stephen Powers wrote in 1877: "(The Hupa) next to the Karok are the finest race in all that region...They are the Romans of Northern California in their valor and their wide-reaching dominions."

The Hupa in this picture are dressed for the White Deer Dance. Powers described it best: "The white deer dance is a dance for luck in which men only participate...They regard the owner of one (white deer skin) as especially favored of the spirits, just as some superstitious people believe him very lucky who finds a four-leafed clover."

Powers offered $100 for a white deerskin but was laughed at. He concluded a Hupa would not sell such a skin at any price but rather see it handed down for use by future generations.

Hupa society recognized a chieftainship whose superior wealth entitled him to lead. As long as the man recognized to be the wealthiest kept his wealth, at his death, his title passed to his son.

The Hupa had a consciousness of a supreme being. They expressed their thoughts and beliefs through their dances. Thus, important expressions evidenced themselves in dances of friendship and of peace. Any person who had an undecided trouble outstanding was prohibited from participating in the Red Woodpecker dance. A special dance celebrated girls reaching puberty, and as important as any was the White Deerskin dance, or luck dance wherein only men participated. Men showed part of their wealth when they displayed a white deerskin, so scarce and hard to hunt successfully, a single pelt might be a man's most valued possession.

Edward Curtis

This Hupa is wearing his White Deerskin Dance *costume.*

Edward Curtis

This Hupa is an obsidian bearer and wears his White Deerskin Dance *costume.*

The men made bows of yew, only about three feet long, strengthened by sinew fastened to the back side of the bow with sturgeon glue. They made their arrows of syringa shoots (mock orange) also wound with sinew.

An arrow could inflict a serious wound at 100 yards, sometimes passing completely through a deer. A hunter would usually prepare for his hunt by ridding himself of some human odors. First he would cleanse himself in a stream and then stand in the path of smoke from a fire of green fir boughs.

Women made beautifully twined baskets and excelled in decorating their dance costumes. Their handwork took the form of

California State University, Humboldt

Hupa Indians at a Yurok town on the Klamath River preparing to dance the Jumping Dance. They wear woodpecker-scalp headbands and carry tubular baskets filled with straw so as to keep their shape. Both this dance and the White Deerskin Dance gave the performers a chance to display their finery and wealth. An albino deer skin without a blemish changed hands for about $200 and attracted admiration.

attaching strings of shell beads, pieces of abalone shells, and obsidian flakes, to their fringed skirts. They wore necklaces of pinenut shells and broken pieces of clam shells. Ordinarily Hupa women wore aprons but in inclement weather to protect its wearer from the cold winds and rains of the Trinity Valley, women (and men) often wore a robe of either deerskin or a wildcat pelt. In rainy weather they wore the skin with the hair side out.

Except for widows, women wore their hair long and tied in queus which hung down in front of their ears. They ornamented them with strips of mink and with pendants of abalone shell. All adult women tattooed themselves with vertical black stripes on their chins.

Lowie Museum, Berkeley, Calif.

This is a fish dam built by the Hupa across the Trinity River. When the salmon crowded up at the dam the natives could spear or net the fish with greater ease. The deep responsibility this tribe felt for all their members is best illustrated by their accommodation each of their two largest towns had for each other. At alternate fishing seasons Takimitlding and Medilding would go without a fish dam that the other might harvest as many salmon as could reach their areas.

The Hupa had acorns and obsidian and some inland foods to trade with their coastal neighbors. In return they received dried seaweed from the coastal people from which they extracted salt. They bought (traded) their dugout canoes from the Yurok at the mouth of the Klamath River.

Edward Curtis

One of the few adult Hupa games was called "stick". Each of two players had about one hundred thin, round, sticks, only one of which had a black band around it. A player put his hands behind his back and divided the sticks in two lots. He held them alongside his thighs while his friends who had bet on him, beat a drum and sang. His opponent would suddenly clap his hands and guess which hand held the black-banded stick. A series of about ten wins determined the winner.

Women gambled in a dice game using two smaller and two larger mussel shell discs to throw.

The lack of roads into the Hupa vastness kept the Indians unaware of the extent of the white man's invasion until about 1850. They were unprepared to find armed white men coming down the South Fork of the Trinity to make their homes. When they did find them misunderstandings and mistakes led to disagreements between both Indians and whites alike. Both thought themselves in the right and reinforced their convictions with deadly force.

Undoubtedly killings took place which never made the pages of the early newspapers. Here is one that did.

Alta California, **May 4, 1852**

"The Shasta Courier of Saturday last contains correspondence from Weaversville, Trinity County, which recounts the particulars of a fearful act of retributive slaughter recently committed in that district. A rancheria of 148 Indians, including women and children, was attacked, and nearly the whole number destroyed.

"It appears that the Indians of that vicinity have for many months displayed uncompromising hostility towards the whites, and several murders and robberies have been daringly perpetrated. About the 15th ultimo, a Mr. Anderson, who was much esteemed in the vicinity of Weaversville, was missed, and a search being made his mutilated remains were found about 6 miles from that place, where he had been attacked by Indians, his cattle driven off, and himself cruelly murdered and robbed. A party of 36 armed men, under Sheriff Dixon pursued the murderers and came up with them on the South Fork of the Trinity. The scene that followed is thus described—

"On Thursday afternoon, the 22nd, the scouts discovered the rancheria in a small valley at the base of 3 mountains on the south side of the South Fork of Trinity River. At midnight the company started from their encampment, Capt. Dixon having divided his force into 3 parties, so as to come upon the Indians from different quarters and surround them. When the day broke, all parties were in the desired positions, and on the signal being given, the attack commenced. Each rifle marked its victim with unerring precision—the pistol and the knife completed the work of destruction and revenge, and in a few moments all was over. Of the 150 Indians that constituted the rancheria, only 2 or 3 escaped, and those were supposed to be dangerously wounded; so that probably not one of those engaged in the murder of the unfortunate Anderson now remains alive. Men, women and children all shared the same fate—none were spared except one woman and two children, who were brought back prisoners.

photo by A. W. Ericson

"Captain" John, a Hupa, is dressed as if for battle. In his left hand he is gripping a typical close combat weapon commonly seen among California tribes. It is a short thrusting spear with an obsidian point.

Under his right arm he carries a quiver made of a whole animal skin. The deerskin wrap, the grass-filled deerskin covered headband, and the dentalium necklaces are typical of Northwestern California Indians. Behind "Captain" John is a sweathouse.

"In palliation of the slaughter of the women and
children it is stated that the Indians thrust them forward as
a screen for themselves, and behind their persons, as from
a barricade, kept up a fire upon their assailants."

The killings went on and were excused by the local authorities.
Settlers sometimes hunted Hupas as they would deer.

The United States established a military post in Hupa territory
in 1855 and maintained it garrisoned until 1892. The soldiers effec-
tively stopped the massacres.

In 1864 the United States created the Hupa Reservation, an area
over twelve miles square, 87,496 acres. It included virtually all of the
Hupa habitat. This, the largest reservation in all of California, had a
population in 1888 said to have been 650 persons on the reservation
and in 1951, 651 persons were reported to be still living there.

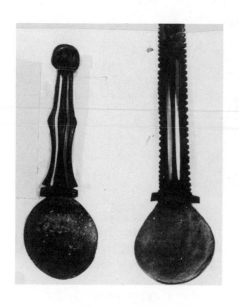

Lowie Museum, Berkeley, Calif.
Hupa elkhorn ladles

Edward Curtis
*This is a Hupa dress worn by
women at ceremonial occasions.*

A law passed in 1988 increased the size of the reservation to 147,740 acres, including much rich timber land. The enlarged sanctuary was split to give both tribes access to their ancestral homes. By virtue of the 1988 legislation some 1,400 Hupa, not all residents of the reservation, were given the heavily timbered 90,000 acres of the reservation known locally as the "Square". Under the same act of Congress about 3,800 Yurok and others with ties to the reservation were allotted at least 10,000 acres along the Klamath River, the home of the most productive salmon fishery.

One thing is obvious when one looks at the Indian population of California, more Hupa and Yurok natives live in freedom on their ancestral homeland than any other tribe in all of the State.

Edward Curtis

This Hupa fisherman is watching for a salmon to leap, intent on gaining ground in the rapids.

33

Lowie Museum, Berkeley, Calif.

This Hupa man is measuring the money remaining on his cord. Such money was dentalium shells. This mollusk lives in sand in comparatively deep water, too deep for California Indians to reach. Vancouver Island Indians fished for them. Dentalium shells reached California by way, in part, of the Klamath River. The Hupa graded their shells very exactly according to length. They are kept on strings that reach from the end of an average man's thumb to the point of his shoulder. The pieces on one string are all of the same size as much as possible. The length of the string was not far from 27 1/2 inches. Dentalium shells of the largest size were exceedingly rare; a string of them might buy a wife for a man of great prominence.

MAIDU

The volcano Mount Lassen erupted often enough in prehistoric times to form the mountain, so it is little wonder the Indians in the northeast corner of California believed the world began there at the desire of a Great Man back when the earth resembled a molten mass. When it cooled, they believed that the deity made a woman to live with him, and from those two came all humans.

Eventually Maidu Indians lived in 74 villages which stretched roughly from the Nevada state line, over the mountains, and down into the low Sacramento Valley foothills, in one place far enough west to include the Marysville Buttes.

The northern Maidu villages were generally south of a line drawn from Susanville west to Mount Lassen. A southern branch of the Maidu, the Nishinam, mainly inhabited the Bear River Valley.

A second belief existed among some Maidu as to their origin. This legend starts with the belief that the tribe once inhabited the Sacramento Valley. One day an immense body of water overcame everyone, and everything in the valley was swept away. This ocean covered the entire valley and allowed only two persons to escape. The Great Man blessed this pair and they produced offspring from which the present people came.

After nine days the Great Man caused a split in a mountain which allowed the valley water to rush out into the ocean. Could this actually be the way the Golden Gate was formed?

Richard Simpson

Maidu baskets were consistently made of willow for the foundation, the root of the hazel nut, the bracken fern, maple and redbud.

While the six dozen villages stretched across well-watered mountains and fertile meadows, the Maidu established themselves in four principal areas: Susanville, Big Meadows (Plumas County), Indian Valley (southeast of Mount Lassen), and American Valley (Feather River).

For the most part the Maidu placed their villages on elevations where approaching strangers could be seen well in advance of their arrival. When, as occasionally happened, villages needed to be built without a view of its approaches, natives manned hilltop posts for their protection.

While each village was self-governed and independent of its neighbors, in practice some three to five villages shared a common hunting territory and fishing streams.

American Museum of Natural History, New York

This is a view of a Maidu summer house. It is made of cut branches tied together and fastened to sapling posts, then covered with brush and often dirt. Inside may be seen baskets for acorn and pine nut storage. Some larger baskets would be used for cooking with hot stones placed in water.

The Maidu built these summer shelters facing east, thus escaping the heat from the hotter afternoon sun rays.

The Maidu made good use of native flora and fauna. They made food gathering the principal springtime activity, often leaving their villages for days or weeks in order to take advantage of ripened volunteer crops somewhere else.

As elsewhere in California, the Maidu chief nut crop was the acorn, with buckeye, nutmeg, and pine nuts being of lesser importance.

As to clothing, the Maidu alone among California tribes wore moccasins, and in winter they wore leggings which reached from the knee to down around the moccasins. The men went naked except for a breechcloth of buckskin worn in winter. The women wore an apron of skin both in front and in back.

For decorations, women pierced their ears and wore bone or wood in them. They attached woodpecker scalps from the bone or wood and often alternated them with the tips of quail scalps.

The Maidu seldom hunted grizzly bears, but when they did, they valued the hide for the warmth it provided them in winter.

Lowie Museum, Berkeley, Calif.

This is a view of a Maidu village near present day Yuba City as it was seen before 1851. It appeared in Gleason's Pictorial Drawing Room Companion, *March 1852. The Sutter Buttes are faithfully pictured in the background.*

38

Men often wore tattoos with patterns of vertical lines on the chin or sometimes a single vertical line rising from the root of the nose. Women tattooed themselves with an odd number of lines on their chins, and occasionally with dots on the backs of their hands.

To decorate themselves in preparation for ceremonials, they used paint made from white and red clay, charcoal, and the grindings of a red stone.

Except for the lower Feather River, navigable rivers didn't exist in Maidu territory. Since they were swift flowing, the natives crossed the lakes in dugout canoes, using either poles or single blade paddles. Occasionally they rode on simple log rafts.

A fraternal feeling among the many villages failed to exist. Grudges between offended individuals sometimes grew into threats and even to warfare between Maidu villages. When one group raided an enemy camp, the enemy usually received warning of the attack before it came. Smoke signals and fire served for the warning. Besides

Lowie Museum, Berkeley, Calif.

This Maidu woman is boiling food using the age-old hot rock system. Using tongs she is about to drop a hot rock she has just taken from the fire. Note the steam rising from the smallest of the three baskets. Note also how large the other two are. This scene was taken near Colfax.

arrows, they fought with sticks, spears, and slings. Male prisoners were usually killed and scalped and the scalps displayed in front of the victors' huts.

The Maidu lived in well watered mountains for hundreds, even thousands of years. They neither decimated the animal life they depended on nor polluted their fishing streams. While violence existed after occasional disagreements, no record of annihilation of one group by another is known.

The mystery of steaming Mount Lassen faced their every generation. Sometimes dormant, appearing to sleep, it sometimes awakened to hide its peak in a plume of vapor, and occasionally its angry gods spewed out death-dealing ash and rock.

The Maidu survived it all—until the white man came to dig up the ground for the yellow metal or brought his hundreds of cattle to graze where the deer had browsed from time immemorial.

Ethnologist Alfred Kroeber estimated that 9,000 Maidu populated their territory before the white invasion. Even the 21 missions had no effect on these people, since more than 100 miles separated them from the closest mission.

Not until 1833, when Hudson Bay Company trappers spent a winter at Marysville Buttes, avoiding the high water of that winter, did any prolonged contact exist between the foreigners and the natives. An epidemic of malaria decimated the natives in that area the same year.

In 1839, Captain John Sutter started building his fort at New Helvetia, now Sacramento. He pressed into his service the most southerly of the Maidu, the Nishinam. The blow from which the Indians never recovered came with the discovery of gold, and from the tens of thousands of foreigners who spread across Maidu territory, beginning in 1848.

By 1850 many streams had been torn up, the fish depleted, and the deer killed off or driven back into the hills so far as to be out of hunting range of the natives. Many Indians went to work for miners and stockmen, given virtually no compensation but second-hand clothing and very little money.

One-third of the native population is reliably estimated to have been alive in 1856. The 1880 count totaled only 2,100, and by 1910 only 1,100 survived. In 1990 Maidu descendants still gather annually for their traditional Bear Dance.

Stephen Powers, Univ. of California Press

The Maidu commonly built their wicker-work granaries near each lodge, sometimes on the ground but more often elevated on stilts, occasionally head-high. The Nishinan, the Maidu's southern neighbors, stored as much as a three year supply of acorns in years of a plentiful harvest.

Some tribes, unlike the Maidu, whose crops of acorns grew at a distance from their lodges, built their granaries where the acorns grew.

Note how completely the granaries are capped. They thus not only keep out birds and squirrels but also shed rain.

An estimate has been made that a typical family of two parents and four children picking acorns for two weeks would probably have gathered 33,500 pounds of the nuts.

There are no accounts of thievery of the granaries' contents and we may conclude the natives respected each others' ownership of them.

Stephen Powers, Univ. of California Press

Since the Maidu inhabited territory all the way from the Sacramento Valley floor to above 7,000 feet in the Sierra, their need for warmer dwelling at the higher elevations made them design their houses for warmth. In this one, the low entrance allows less heat to escape than would a conventional entrance. Also, being constructed of slabs it provides good insulation.

Dorsy

This Maidu lady from the Grass Valley area has nearly completed her basket in which she used an intricate design.

WINTUN AND PATWIN

In a general pattern the Indians of the Copehan family, groups with linguistic similarities, occupied the Sacramento Valley from Mt. Shasta to Suisun Bay. While they lived along the Sacramento River, they seldom made their villages more than a mile or two from the east bank. However, on the west they established themselves from the river to the Coast Range.

The two principal divisions, the Wintun and the Patwin, spoke similar words in only about one-third of their vocabulary. Yet anthropologist Alfred L. Kroeber in his 1976 *Handbook of the Indians of California* grouped them together. More specifically, Kroeber divides them into four divisions, Northern, Central, Southeastern, and Southwestern Wintun. The latter included the most southerly Patwin villages, those facing Suisun Bay. Those in the Napa Valley were unusual. They spoke the language of their neighbors as well as their own.

Their favorite amusement consisted of gathering for ceremonies and dances. The ritual involved did solemnize the occasions, but even without it the Wintun enjoyed being together for a good time.

They ate so well that the Wintun tended to obesity. Food was usually plentiful. But compared to most California Indians they were considered poor hunters. This may have been because fishing could be so successful. They were considered excellent fishermen. Not only the Sacramento River but also the scores of tributaries which ran into it supplied them with the reason to excel in fishing.

43

They ate some foods raw, such as manzanita berries, some leaves and even a few stems.

They steamed many bulbs, and they roasted roots, tubers and grasshoppers.

They parched most seeds. The two most important to their diet were the sunflower and the Clarkia seeds. To a lesser degree they collected hazel, sugar-pine and digger-pine nuts and a variety of berries and fruits.

In Autumn the natives collected buckeye nuts, which they hulled and leached, but because the buckeye is unstable they ate them soon after harvest.

As elsewhere in California the Indians depended on acorns for their principal supply of food.

From Alexander Forbes, *A History of Lower & Upper California*, 1877
This is the interior of a central California sweathouse or temescal, undoubtedly earth covered, as seen by Forbes.

The Wintun were not only fond of bathing in cold water, but would dive into a river and remain long enough to fill their mouths with clams and come up only after filling both hands with them too.

The Wintun speared their fish with a spear often fifteen feet long. A fisherman would locate himself above a vantage point, looking down into the current, waiting for a fish to come his way. He would stand for a long time, without moving, patiently waiting for his quarry to flash by beneath him.

Wintun fishermen were so capable that they dried more fish than they could use. They would often trek into the mountains seeking Maidu who would trade bows made of cedar for dried salmon.

Drawn by Henry B. Brown, John Carter Brown Univ. Library, Providence, Rhode Island
These are probably Wintun Indians enjoying a social evening of gambling in their sweathouse. Note entrance is gained through a hole in the roof. The upright pole adjacent to the hole is climbed when exiting the sweathouse. Undoubtedly a stream or lake is only a few steps away, for the Indian must douse himself in cold water to complete the advantage of his sweatbath. In addition he wants to wash away all human scent to have the advantage in case he goes hunting.

Researcher Sherburne F. Cook has estimated that only about 10% of the California Indian population remained alive by 1900.

What happened to the Wintun?

Early on the mission Indians caught the diseases from the soldiers and settlers who accompanied Portolá and Anza in the first decade of their occupation of California. But most Wintun had virtually no contact with the missions The Patwin villages which faced Suisun Bay did have occasional contact with Europeans before construction commenced on Mission San Francisco Solano at Sonoma, in the summer of 1823. Yet the Wintun escaped epidemics until ten years later.

Stephen Powers, Univ. of California Press

Wailaki girls were usually tattooed between the ages 15-17. Though they could be betrothed before puberty most often the promise to marry meant no more than that—it could easily be broken. Brides were purchased and the price was negotiable. At birthing the Wailaki cut the naval cord using a flint blade. Members of this tribe avoided marriage with kin, a practice not often adhered to by neighboring groups.

Natives in the central and northern Wintun territory saw their first European in 1821.

That year, the last Spanish expedition in America and the first of any Europeans into Northern Sacramento Valley, under the command of Luis Arguello, went up into Wintun territory in October and November. This first group to possibly leave a European disease among these California natives crossed Carquinez Straits and trekked north along the western side of the Sacramento Valley as far as Stony Creek. There they turned west, ultimately returning to Monterey, by way of Stonyford and Middletown.

Six years later, in 1827, a more consistent social intercourse commenced when the British-owned Hudson Bay Company sent brigades of French and American trappers farther and farther afield, following Jedediah Smith's trip of exploration that year.

The Hudson Bay trappers set up a base camp which they used for about ten years at what became known as French Camp, San Joaquin County.

They trapped in all directions from there, leaving in 1839 after they had exterminated the beaver.

From J. R. Bartlett, 1854, Univ. of California Press

Patwin Indians fishing with a boom net. During the salmon run this type net caught substantial quantities of fish with little effort.

Stephen Powers, 1877, Univ. of California Press

California Indians used their sweathouses on almost a daily basis just as we take showers today. It didn't serve for medicinal purposes but rather for social reasons, a sort of men's club. In addition, before going out hunting men used the sweathouse to remove as much human scent as possible that they might creep as close as possible, undetected, to their quarry. Just before leaving the temescal they scraped their bodies clean of perspiration with a blade about a foot long, made of the lower jaw of a porpoise. Every village had at least one temescal, some had more.

Nevertheless, in 1833, a major smallpox epidemic hit several Sacramento Valley tribes. The Wintun lost about 10% of their number that year. In 1838 they lost hundreds more to another smallpox plague. Still another pestilence, an unknown fever (cholera or scarlet fever) hit the Wintun tribe. In all, Sherburne Cook estimated Northern California tribes lost 60% of their population to the diseases to which they had little immunity. Cook calculated that this was five times the number as were killed by homicides in the same time. On that basis, between disease and homicide they would account for 72% of the natives living in 1832 who were dead by 1850.

Edward Curtis

Gathering tule, an age old task, one of scores delegated exclusively to women.

What reduced the Indian inhabitants even more, particularly in Northern California after 1850, is illustrated by the several newspaper articles which follow. Hundreds more can by culled from the publications of the times and there must have been thousands of shootings which were never reported. This sampling will give the reader an idea of how frail the life of a Wintun became after the settlers moved in, fenced land, and told the natives to stay out. Kroeber estimated about 1,000 Wintun were still living in 1923, and that the peak population of the tribe had been 12,000.

By this time (1850-1870) the United States Army fostered an almost paternalistic attitude toward much of the Indian population, except in Northwestern California. Particularly in Del Norte and Humboldt Counties, settlers hounded the military through the press to exterminate the natives for their stealing of livestock. At the same time more civilized elements of the white population sometimes called the military murderers for their acts of reprisal in spite of their reluctance to take action. Little evidence exists however to show the Army took an active interest in preventing the settlers' annihilation of the natives.

Edward Curtis

The Modoc made their balsa canoes with a square stern unlike the Indians elsewhere in California. Their habitat included the following waterways: Goose Lake, Little Klamath Lake, Modoc Lake, Tule Lake and the streams in Lost River Valley.

Alta California, April 19, 1851

Near Cottonwood, the Indians have been punished severely by the citizens. On the evening that Mr. Curtis camped at Leonard's ranch, just on this side of the stream, a company of men returned from the pursuit of the thieves. They had killed that day about 30, assisted by some friendly "Diggers" of the Valley. Mr. Curtis heard the relation of the affair and says the citizens gave the "Diggers" great credit for the manner of their bearing in the fight...

San Francisco Chronicle, March 29, 1854

Col. W. Miller, Commander of the American Forces at Fort Brown, near Shasta, furnishes us with the following particulars of an encounter at Yreka Pass: On the 25th ult, with a command of 72, officers and men, they pursued the savages into the above-mentioned Pass, near the Oregon line. On reaching the northern end of the Pass, the Indians, in a body numbering about 500 strong, made a most bold and vigorous attack; but were repulsed after a well-con-

Edward Curtis

This Indian lady, dressed in cloth clothes, probably in the late 1800s, is still collecting seeds for food, by beating ripened seeds into her collecting basket

tested fight, with the loss of 60 or 70, and driven into the mountains.

Marysville Weekly Express, April 15, 1859

A new plan has been adopted by our neighbors opposite this place to chastise the Indians for their many depredations during the past winter. Some men are hired to hunt them, who are recompensed by receiving so much for each scalp, or some other satisfactory evidence that they have been killed. (Twenty-five cents was the customary bounty.)

Marysville Appeal, February 8, 1861

Several hundred miserable Indians have been slain in Tehama, Mendocino and Humboldt Counties, during the past eighteen months, and hundreds during the years preceding, for the hunger offense of cattle stealing. It appears by the proceedings of a recent meeting of stock raisers, held at the Nome Lackee Reservation, and which proceedings we find in the Red Bluff Independent, that there are many white men who take their neighbor's stock, and have nothing worse hurled at them, therefore; but a string of resolutions.

San Francisco Bulletin, July 12, 1862

There are at present at Fort Humboldt about 350 Indian prisoners, three quarters of them squaws and children. They can hardly be considered "trophies of war", as the greater portion were not captured but came in voluntarily—influenced so to do, doubtless, by ascertaining that the captives at the fort had good rations and a "good time" generally.

Of the "fighting Indians", our troops in their various encounters thus far have killed some 70 or 80, but have very rarely succeeded in taking any of them prisoners, as, after exchanging a few shots, those who are not killed or very badly wounded, escape into the thickets, where it is generally impossible to overtake them. Our men have been but seldom hit, owing in part to the superiority of range of our arms (rifle muskets), and partly to the fact that generally, by night marches our scouts have been enabled to surprise them in their camps.

I fear that the perusal of this long story may weary the readers of the Bulletin, but I could not refrain from stating the facts regarding our operations here, and the various difficulties we are called upon to encounter, hoping that the "reading public" will be convinced that the 2d Infantry Cavalry Vol. and other troops in this District have been and are doing their whole duty.

Sacramento Daily Union, June 11, 1863

Five Indians were found suspended to a hydraulic flume, at Helltown (Butte Co.). The Indians have been suspected of committing several depredations lately, robbing cabins and running off horses. The 5 Indians were captured, bound and held as prisoners for 2 or 3 days by the citizens. It is not known whether they confessed to any crime, but it is certain the "Captain" and 4 of his tribe suffered the extreme punishment of Judge Lynch.

Yreka Semi-Weekly Union, March 26, 1864

The new military commandant of the district, Col. Black, is doing good service in Indian hunting. He keeps his troops in the mountains most of the time scouting, and has introduced a new method of treating hostile Indian prisoners—hangs them all. That style of dealing with a murdering Digger is very effective, and meets with universal approval by the citizen inhabitants of the hostile region. It seems to be a general sentiment here that a mean "Digger" only becomes a "good Indian" when he is dangling from the end of a rope, or has an ounce of lead in him.

Humboldt Times, May 5, 1855

Colonel Henley has been endeavoring to discover persons engaged in the nefarious trade of stealing Indians. A large number of children have been brought down and sold in the agricultural counties. They bring from $50 to $250 each.

The *Petaluma Journal* of April 15, 1857, says that extensive Indian killing has taken place, and still is occurring in the vicinity of Round Valley. Information has been received in Petaluma, through a gentleman just from there, that within the past three weeks, from 300 to 400 bucks, squaws and children have been killed by the whites.

Stephen Powers, Univ. of California Press

The dome-shaped lodge was the most popular in California. On the Sacramento and San Joaquin Valley plains the natives covered the thatched dome with the most common insulating material they had, earth. In the one pictured here the entrance was reached by the steps to the hole in the roof. More common may have been the door on either the east or the north side. This one is probably a Patwin lodge.

POMO

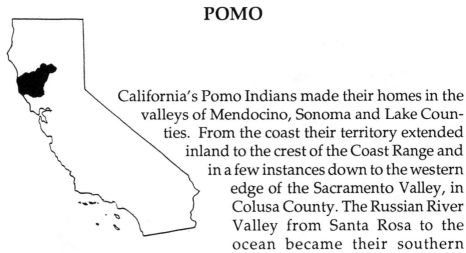

California's Pomo Indians made their homes in the valleys of Mendocino, Sonoma and Lake Counties. From the coast their territory extended inland to the crest of the Coast Range and in a few instances down to the western edge of the Sacramento Valley, in Colusa County. The Russian River Valley from Santa Rosa to the ocean became their southern boundary.

Their northern limit began about twenty miles north of Ft. Bragg and continued easterly across the Eel River to and including Clear Lake.

They built their huts in villages where all members were related. 479 such villages have been identified by name. Of this large number 75 can be called principal villages, because a chief or chiefs lived there. Thus these chiefs controlled an average of about seven settlements each. Their duties included organizing food gathering expeditions, settling family disputes, and ending hostilities after conflict broke out.

In some of the larger Pomo villages, two chiefs shared responsibilities: one a war-chief and the other a peace-chief. The latter concerned himself with the spiritual needs of his people. The war-chief made decisions involving food, politics and day-to-day disputes. When the war-chief became elderly he replaced the peace-chief who stepped down.

Except in winter the Pomo men wore no clothing. In the cold months they wore a cloak, without sleeves, which hung loosely from their shoulders. They made them of either redwood or willow bark or in areas where it grew profusely, shredded tule.

The women wore a skirt of whatever material was available where they lived. Along the coast they used shredded redwood bark; along the rivers, shredded willow bark; and around the lakes they used tule.

Originally these brown-skinned natives were a peaceful people. They were gentle and clever artisans. They made beads of clam shells and with the never-ending supply of the shells they used them as trade goods with interior villages. The women wore ornaments of bird bones, some elaborate and some delicate.

Lowie Museum, Berkeley, Calif.

This is a traditional Pomo dance house. The roof of this house would be held up by probably six oak posts each about one foot in diameter. Oak stringers, each 6 to 8 inches in diameter were then laid horizontally from one large post to the next. Above them and radiating from the peak to the edge of the roof would be heavy rafters, usually of cottonwood or willow. Topping off the roof, this house has split shakes. In early times the Pomos topped off their roofs with a thatch of cottonwood boughs, willow branches and grass. Before the whites came to California the Indians made their dance houses semi-subterranean by digging out a pit several feet in depth for their floor level.

Of the almost 500 Pomo settlements only about 25 occupied coastal land while the others were located in valleys or beside streams. Those along streams were placed on the north or east side so as to capitalize on the sunshine and the more abundant vegetation. Each community also had a range of hills under its control.

Men averaged five feet five inches in height; the women were shorter. Both genders tattooed themselves, the men on the face and nose, and the women on breasts and abdomen.

Most often both men and women were fat and had large faces. They were peaceful and dreamed of the perfect life in heaven above. They knew they would someday ascend to it by way of a ladder. They believed the wicked among them would fall from their ladder down

Lowie Museum, Berkeley, Calif.
This is a Pomo sweathouse which existed in Lake County. In addition to acting as a sauna would today men also used it for sleeping in winter time. With the fire out, they had the benefit of the warmth retained by this well insulated house. Beside the earth covered roof, the semi-subterranean structure had a narrow entrance.

This may have been one of the last Pomo foot drums in existence. It stands 6 to 7 feet high and is made of a peeled and hollowed out Sycamore log. It provided accompaniment for the dancers.

Behind the drum is a semi-subterranean dance house which was the center of the social, religious, and political life of the village. All important gatherings and ceremonies were held here.

Nearly all their acts of worship were held in honor of reptiles, beasts or birds. Certain of their dances were solemn and austere.

While there is no doubt the Pomo believed in a Supreme Being he seemed to have negative attributes. Like many other California tribes the Pomo knew the Coyote created both the world and mankind.

into a void, an extraordinary nothing, where they would roam without thought or purpose forever. The most wicked would turn into grizzlies or rattlesnakes and have to crawl on hot scorching earth without end. To every Pomo hell was a place where he was forever hungry.

The Pomo believed in a Supreme Being called Cha-kal-le, "The Great One". They worshipped the coyote and believed he was the Creator of the world and everything on it.

One coyote legend which now seems to have no definition or reason behind it nevertheless persisted. It involved a man with two sons, all three of them very wicked. Because of their deeds they were turned into coyotes. The three of them journeyed into Potter Valley where one son drank so much water he died. His father buried him under a heap of stones and mourned for him.

The man and his remaining son went on to Clear Lake where the second son drank so much water he died too. His father buried him and wept over his grave.

The old man started back the way he came and came to a place where he discovered a large deposit of red alabaster, a material the Pomo made beads of. Suddenly the father's hair came out and his tail dropped off his body and then he stood up and turned into a man.

The Pomo believed Coyote to be the first being in existence. In their mythology he remained the single most important character. He played two roles. The first was a culture hero and the second was as a trickster. As the deity the Pomo called him Iwi'Madú'mda.

As the culture hero, Coyote created most if not all the universe. One of the Pomo myths tells how Coyote created the ocean.

Lowie Museum, Berkeley, Calif.
This Pomo basketry fish trap was a common type among California Indians. A popular length was five feet.

Coyote wished the ocean would come into existence and roll up against the shore furiously. Before this there was no ocean and the land was even all along its edge. At once, after Coyote made this wish the great water appeared and came rolling in, in great waves against the shore. It came so hard that it tore away a lot of the land and made the present rough shoreline.

When Coyote saw how rough it was he became afraid and made the water roll in more gently and be more calm so that anyone could walk out in it and get mussels, abalones, seaweeds, and all the different kinds of sea foods that we now eat.

Another myth is about how Coyote created Thunder. Coyote, the Creator, went from Mount Kanaktai to Sanhedrim Mountain and from there he went across to Redwood Mountain.

On this high mountain he created Thunder and sent him from there to the coast to Big River where he now lives in a house under the water.

Thunder always comes from the west to the east and returns. This is the origin of the sound which emanates from this house at Big River and always returns to the same place.

Another Pomo belief involves the grizzly bear. They believe every grizzly is some old savage Indian returned to the world to be punished for his wickedness.

Marriage was conducted by the peace-chief in a formal ceremony. The bridegroom had earlier satisfied the bride's parents by making them a generous present such as a fine pelt or deer skins. A merry-making party with dancing and eating followed the ceremony. The bride went off with her husband to live with his family. There he was an experienced hunter and fisherman and already a proven provider.

In some groups the men prohibited the women from learning the dialect of a neighboring tribelet so that their wives wouldn't go gadding about or seeking an affair with a strange man.

While the aged who died were most often buried it was not unknown for a man or woman to dig his or her own grave. In many cases, after completing it, they sat on the edge of the hole for weeks or even months at a time, and in that position they ate such meals as they were given.

Smithsonian Institution
Pomo man holding his bow in the shooting position. The two arrows for his next shots are between his teeth and the remainder are in the animal skin quiver under his arm. His armor consists of rods of willow or hazel shoots closely twined with cordage, in two layers, an outer vertical one, and an inner horizontal one.

Stephen Powers, Univ. of California Press

These two Pomos are pulling in their nets in an eastern arm of Clear Lake. They built communal, three or four families to a dwelling, huts on Rattlesnake Island.

In the event a tribelet or family desired to travel to or through another Pomo settlement or to gather food in an area not considered their own, correct manners called for the travelers to send a messenger ahead asking for permission. Failing this protocol might cause resentment possibly resulting in an armed conflict.

Lowie Museum, Berkeley, Calif.

These five Eastern Pomo dancers are about to recreate the New Ghost Dance. In its original form the dance promoted Indian self-esteem. The ceremony went so far as to promise its believers the white invaders (settlers) would be wiped out by a natural disaster and the Indians would thus be able to return to their traditional ways.

The Pomo living along the coast built a warmer hut than their inland brethren. They split redwood logs into slabs from six to eight feet long. They stood them on end, leaning inward at the top. Thus their dwellings looked like upside down cones. They laid long strips of redwood bark against the slabs which gave them considerable insulation.

Inland the natives built both round dome-shaped huts or rectangular ones. In both cases they first made a framework of willow branches they bent into the desired shape. They bent them to form a dome and where the branches met they tied them using vines for rope. Once they finished making the frame the Indians thatched and wove between the uprights with tule and grass. They wove mats which they hung on the inside door frame.

Each village had its sweat house. The Indians used them for both medicinal and ceremonial purposes. During the winter men and boys spent considerable time in the village sweat house.

C. Hart Merriam described one use of these houses:

> "It was the custom of the men to go to these homes twice a day, morning and evening. Each man carried a log or an armful of sticks for the large fire. The heat soon became very intense. When the men had stood it as long as they could, they ran out, lay on the ground awhile to cool off, then plunged into the river.

> "The men were divided into two parties or sides— one on the north, the other on the south.

> "While the men are lying on the ground in the heat of the sweathouse, a man from each side, provided with a pole to which is attached a deerskin or blanket, steps to the other side and fans the heat against his opponents, the effort being to make the place so hot that it cannot be endured. When a man runs out, unable to stand it any longer, his side is declared vanquished, the other side the winners."

J. R. Bartlett, 1854

This is the interior of a Northern California Indian dwelling. Note the set of duck decoys and seed gathering baskets as well as the baby cradle.

All the major villages had a separate dance house. Today we would call it the town hall. The natives used it to hold religious ceremonies, social events, and such political meetings as they had need for.

The Smithsonian Institution's Bureau of Ethnology in its report covering all the tribes north of Mexico credit the Pomo women with, "They are noted for their basketry, which in variety of technique and range of patterns is probably unrivaled in North America, while its fineness of finish and elaborateness of decoration, especially with feathers, are remarkable." (Bulletin #30, 1907, page 277)

The women made both coiled and twined baskets. The latter was usually so tightly coiled that it could be used for holding liquids without any leakage. In coiled baskets they used more decorations. For color they used bright feathers. Other decorative materials included shells and beads.

In making baskets the women used willow, redbud bark, bullrush root, and Digger Pine root fibers.

While brightly-colored feathers were prized by the basket makers for ornamenting their baskets, probably the most universally used feather was the top-knot of the California Quail.

While the Pomo people were considered a peaceful group, the natives of the Santa Rosa Valley were the more warlike of the tribe. Their proximity to the Californians of Mexican descent had a bearing on why this southern group lost so many lives to superior arms.

The last mission to be built was at Sonoma, San Francisco Solano. When it opened in 1823 the mission fathers brought Indians from San Francisco, San Rafael, and San Jose, 693 of them.

In 1834 the Mexican Government took control of the missions out of the hands of the priests and turned it over to the locally appointed authority. General Mariano G. Vallejo represented the

John Le Baron

Some examples of Pomo basketry, both coiled and twined baskets, two of ten Pomo techniques.

California Governor in that capacity in Sonoma. He also commanded the Mexican soldiers stationed there.

Vallejo turned the command of the troops over to his brother, Salvador, a man who hated the Indians.

In a fight with some Santa Rosa Indians several of his soldiers were killed, and the survivors fled, the Indians victorious.

Not long after this defeat, a runaway mission native stole one of General Vallejo's mules. He sent an Indian after him but the man fell into the hands of the tribe who had defeated Salvador Vallejo in the recent battle. They tortured him and when Salvador heard the news he vowed revenge.

Vallejo returned with a larger force and this time defeated them, making slaves of three hundred and killing eight hundred of them, according to him.

While Salvador Vallejo was a brutal man and undoubtedly caused the death of several thousand natives, his actions were minor compared to the number who died of diseases brought to them by the Mexicans and Americans. Gen. Mariano G. Vallejo made the estimate of between 60,000 and 75,000 deaths within his jurisdiction alone in the epidemic of 1838. Ten years earlier a smallpox plague spread through all the California missions carrying off untold numbers of the natives.

It is little wonder the numbers of the Pomos left alive was small when the Americans crossed the mountains and made their homes among the surviving Indians. After the Gold Rush, the natives lived peacefully beside the newcomers. While many Indians worked as farm hands, doing seasonal work for the whites, others farmed for themselves or worked on the few tribal communities left intact.

It was a fact that many Americans refused to hire any Indians, especially men, who were denied the chance to buy the necessities of life for a family, having a devastating effect on keeping the family together. Contributing to the problem was the ability of some women to hire out as domestics while their husbands could not contribute their share.

Lowie Museum, Berkeley, Calif.

This Pomo lady in the Ukiah Valley in recent times has roasted caterpillars as a delicacy for her female relatives.

In years of scarcity, toasted grasshoppers were added to meals. Most of the time acorns filled the need of their basic diet.

Lowie Museum, Berkeley, Calif.

This is a Pomo cache for storing acorns. All tribes had some kind of store structure for storing seeds or beans as well as acorns, and very few tribes seemed to have similar shapes for their caches.

This coastal Pomo lady is beating the ripened seeds using her concave shaped wicker beater. Her basket is the large conical shape which was used virtually everywhere in California.

Lowie Museum, Berkeley, Calif.

This Pomo basket maker is from the Ukiah rancheria. While most California Indians appreciated fine baskets and most made admirable ones, Pomo basketry may have been the epitome of the art. Even visiting tribesmen admired the finely woven, feather-decorated, delicate handiwork of the Pomo, having seldom seen their equal anywhere else.

Lowie Museum, Berkeley, Calif.

POMO

Viola Roseberry

These are rare old Pomo wedding and meal baskets. The two smaller ones are utility trays. All are made from red fir and rosebud root.

A branch of the great Pomo nation, the Gallinomero, once occupied Dry Creek Valley and the Russian River Valley below Healdsburg. Their chiefs inherited their titles. Probably their last chief, Ventura, lived in this lodge with twenty to thirty of his tribelet.

All along the middle of the lodge each family had its own fire. They slept next to the walls, lying on the ground under rabbit skin robes.

There were three narrow holes for doors, one at either end and one at the elbow.

The Gallinomero were so dark as to be almost black, with lips rather thick and sensual, and with a low forehead. One observer noted them to have "a sluggish but foggy expression."

COAST MIWOK

So much has been written about the Coast Miwok and how they lived and how they were treated *after* they saw their first Spanish missionary and Spanish soldier, it is worthwhile considering what those who came to California 200 years *before* the missionaries and soldiers had to say about them.

The Miwok in Marin County became the first Indians in all of California to live for a while with white men. For five weeks, in the summer of 1579, they brought food and firewood to Francis Drake, the Englishman who beached his ship, the *Golden Hinde*, in what we now call Drake's Bay. He turned his ship on one side to clean off the bottom, then turned it over and did the same on the other side, scraping off the seaweed and barnacles which had slowed down his sailing time.

Drake's report to Queen Elizabeth has been lost. The descriptions of the Indians living near Drake's landing place come from the only two literate men, beside Drake himself, on board the *Golden Hinde*, ship chaplain Francis Fletcher and Drake's nephew, John Drake.

J. W. Robertson
Francis Drake sailed the Golden Hinde *into Drake's Bay in June 1579. He lived with the Coast Miwok for five weeks, the first European the Indians had ever seen*

"The men for the most part go naked the women take a kind of bulrushes, and kembing [combing?] it after the manner of hemp make themselves thereof a loose garment, which being knitte about their middles, hangs downe about their hippes, affords them a covering, having also about their shoulders a skinne of Deere, with the hair upon it.

"...their houses are digged round within the earth and have from the uttermost brimmes of the circles clefts of wood set up, and joyned close together at the top like our spires on the steeple of a church; which being covered with earth, suffer no water to enter, and are very warme; the door in most part of them performs the office also of a chimney to let out the smoke.

"The king had on his head a cawle of knit-work, wrought upon somewhat like the crownes;...his guards also having cawles likewise stuck with feathers, or crowned over with a certain downe, which groweth up in the country an herbe much like our letuce, which exceeds any other downe in fineness, and being laid upon their cawles, can by no wind be removed."

Net caps filled with down were described as, "crownes made of knitwork, wrought upon most curiously with feathers of divers colours, very artificially placed, and of a formal fashion.

"Their baskets were made in a fashion like a deep boale, and though the matters were rushes, or such other kind of stuffe, yet was it so cunningly handled, that the most part of them would hold water; about the brimmes they were hanged with peeces of shels of pearles [broken bits of abalone shell?] and in some places with two or three linkes at a place; and besides this, they were wrought upon with matted downe of red feathers.

"...our General with his company traveled up into the Country to their villages, where we found herds of Deere by 1,000 in a company, being most large [probably elk], and fat of body."

From Arnoldus Montanus, *Die unbekante neue Welt*; the Dapper issue, Amsterdam, 1673

The first European to land in California was Juan Rodriguez Cabrillo who went ashore in Southern California in 1542. The earliest European to visit Northern California was Francis Drake who landed on the Marin County coast of California in June, 1579.

All accounts which survived his voyage emphasize that the Coast Miwok Indians received the commander as they would a deity. Throughout his five-week stay the natives remained both peaceful and friendly.

At the time of his departure the accounts agree, there was much weeping, after seeing their wishes for the Englishmen to remain had failed the Indians.

In 1599, twenty years after Francis Drake visited the Pt. Reyes Peninsula, Theodor de Bry produced this engraving depicting the welcome the Coast Miwok Indians gave the explorer. While much is fanciful, including the two ships, the Golden Hinde *came alone. The quiver is genuine. The chief in a headdress and with a deer-skin loin cloth are what we might expect him to be wearing. The nakedness of most of the natives is certainly correctly depicted. The weeping woman at the right apparently fears for the safety of her family as they cower around the fire in spite of the momentous scene going on around them. The conical slab huts were undoubtedly used in a place as fog-bound as Drake's Bay. The Indians undoubtedly rushed over the hills to see a sailing ship and men from another world for the first time. The two closest major villages were one at Olema and a larger one at Nicasio.*

The Coast Miwok lived in 44 villages but not in any on the Point Reyes Peninsula. The two largest were probably those at Olema and Nicasio. Others were near Tomales Bay, at Marshall, Dillon Beach, and Tomales. Others in or near San Francisco Bay were at Bolinas, Sausalito, Ignacio, and three along San Rafael's shoreline.

The natives who lived inland built five villages along Petaluma Creek, four near Sonoma, three at Freestone, two at Bodega and two along San Antonio Creek.

Many Coast Miwok favored Bodega Bay where they lived in seven villages. The total aboriginal population has been estimated by authorities to have been only 2,000 which translates to only 45 persons per village on average.

Small groups of unrelated Miwok also populated the area across Carquinez Straits: Martinez to Walnut Creek. Others lived on Sherman Island and along the Sacramento River almost as far north as Sacramento itself.

Each of 6 to 10 persons slept in their conical or grass covered huts. They slept with their feet toward the fire on mats spread on the ground with grass pillows under their heads.

Aside from an occasional dispute between families the Marin County natives had little reason to go to war. They had plenty of food and a moderate climate. They gathered seeds, acorns and buckeye from the land, snared waterfowl with slings or bolas from creeks and lakes, and collected mussels, clams, crab, and kelp along the shoreline.

Seldom did they resort to hunting bear and elk. Deer were everywhere and frequently fell victim to the bow and arrow. They gave their bows extra strength by wrapping the central section with sinew taken from the wing of a brown pelican. When they shot game they shot a long arrow with three feathers in the end strung to a sinew cord. These arrows had only a sharpened point, not an obsidian one.

They caught their fish in several ways, in a sock-like wicker trap, in weirs, with spears and using dip nets often made from the lupine root. According to the strength required they would twist two or three strands of the root into a stronger rope.

Louis Choris, 1816

Choris identifies the women on the left and the center as from a Coast Miwok tribelet in Marin County, the one second from the left a Utschuin, an Alameda County tribelet, and the two on the right as Saklans, a Miwok family group in the Walnut Creek area. Over 160 Saklan were baptized at Mission Dolores between 1794-1810. The artist left us this observation of the natives: "I have never seen one laugh. I have never seen one look one in the face. They look as though they were interested in nothing."

This is how the Coast Miwok natives were described almost 200 years ago. The drawings in these pages were made undoubtedly from these descriptions and may have been embellished by comments from the first hand observers at the time.

One year before the San Francisco Presidio and the Mission Dolores were established, the first ship to enter the Golden Gate, the *San Carlos*, sailed in and soon visited some Coast Miwok living on the north shore of San Francisco Bay.

The Commander of the expedition, Frigate-Lieutenant Don Juan de Ayala left some notes about his visit to the North Bay.

"...right from the first day's dealings with the Indians...it was obvious at once how friendly they were...they explained to them by signs that they would be able to eat and sleep there [either Angel Island or the Tiburon shore]. They had already prepared for them on the shore a present of pinole-gruel, bread made of their seeds, and tamales of the same.

"When at the passage on the northeastern side, a channel a mile and a half wide, deep and clear, lies into the land. At the eastern side of its entrance is situated a village of more than 400 souls...gave them presents with the beads...and some used clothing...because of the quantity of presents they made us very rich fish, the salmon among them and their seeds and pinole-gruel, and what is more, great decency and propriety in their women. They are in nowise demanding things."

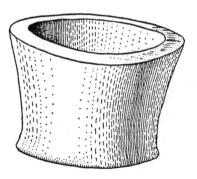

Robert F. Heizer, Univ. of California Press
This is a drawing of a basalt mortar. Archeological diggings at Drake's Bay have uncovered a score of similar utensils. Since there are no basalt deposits in the area any closer than 25 miles, and since each weighed from 20 to 125 pounds, transporting them to where they were found must have been a heavy task for the barefoot Indians. The question arises, why would there be so many large mortars at Drake's Bay? Could they have been taken there at the time of Drake's visit?

C. H. Merriam

This is a tall-roofed Miwok roundhouse. A large one such as this would be between 50 and 60 feet in diameter and the interior would be a few feet below the surrounding ground level. Ceremonial dancers would be dressed in elaborately decorated costumes with much use of bird feathers. A drum 6 to 7 feet long, made of a peeled and hollowed out sycamore provided accompaniment for the dancers. Many ceremonies had religious significance and acknowledged the native's dependence on nature for their sustenance.

Robert F. Heizer

Tule weed grows in marshy ground to a height of six to ten feet or more. Its air-filled hollow core makes it buoyant. The Indians cut down the tules and tied them in bundles and then tied the bundles into the canoe pictured here. This boat could easily carry a load of 300 to 400 pounds. In many cases water would sooner or later begin to seep through the tules and the occupants accepted the inevitable. When beyond use, water-logged, they either sank or were just abandoned.

The Coast Miwok observed the usual practice of virtually all California Indians, their land belonged to the group. However, they did observe an individual's right to some of the food producing trees, such as oak and buckeye. So too did they consider the private property of an individual to clam-digging rights, even to some hunting and fishing areas.

The Coast Miwok had no overall tribal organization. Only the larger villages had a chief and his duties were principally to see that his villagers acted for the best interests of all. It has been said he harangued his people every day, giving advice applicable to all. Large villages often had two women leaders. One prepared the villagers for their important dances while the second woman bossed the construction of new ceremonial houses and sent out invitations to the celebrations to neighboring villages. The Indians held dances whenever possible. They danced and made music before going on a hunt for big game, celebrating their youth, becoming men, observing the funeral rites of an important member of their tribe, and before going to war.

The Coast Miwok lived their traditional, peaceful way of life until they saw a ship's boat going up Petaluma Creek on a day in September, 1775. Accompanying the boat was a land party of Spanish soldiers. While the Mission Dolores in San Francisco was only under construction the Spaniards were out searching for natives to lure across the bay, by presents or by force, to inhabit the new mission.

The Coast Miwok were so slow to cross the Golden Gate for the first few years after Mission Dolores opened that none received baptism for eight years. The first to be christened was a six year old, who received the rites in 1783.

Some of the natives from north of the bay stayed away from Mission Dolores and others went over to stay for several years. Many early deaths, almost of panic proportions, occurred in the early 1800s and by 1817 the mission authorities decided to build a mission at San Rafael. When completed it served Mission Dolores as a sanitarium to send their ill, who suffered mostly from pulmonary causes.

By 1820, 590 neophytes *belonged* to Mission San Rafael and about half of them were transferees from Mission Dolores. The maximum population, 1,140, lived at San Rafael in 1828.

The Indian men worked in the granary and in the several workshops. They tended cattle and sheep and cut timber, whipsawing logs into boards for the mission's needs.

Along Tomales Bay, up to Bodega Bay, the natives kept closer to their original habits, feeling less pressure to join the missions at both San Rafael and Sonoma. Nevertheless the epidemics of 1833 and 1838 reached them also, killing many of the Coast Miwoks in both places.

In 1834, when the missions were abandoned by the church, the missionaries distributed their livestock among the Indians. At San Rafael, beside the cattle, 343 Indians were dealt out 1,291 sheep and 439 horses.

Lowie Museum, Berkeley, Calif.
These three coast Miwok are on their way to a day of gathering wild seeds. Note the wide mouth baskets in the stern of their balsa. The Marin shoreline is in the background.

At Sonoma they felt less secure in private ownership of live-stock and ultimately asked General Guadalupe M. Vallejo to care for the herd for them. This Vallejo did according to the record, treating the animals as the Indians' property.

When the Americans took up land in Marin and Sonoma Counties in the late 1840s, many remaining Indians went to work for them in dairying, lumbering, and in agriculture.

The 1852 census tallied 250 Indians still living in Coast Miwok country. The 1880 census accounted for only 60 and eight years later the count was only 6 full-blooded Coast Miwok still alive.

However, even in 1990 many mixed-blood Coast Miwok still weave traditional baskets and perform some of the customary dances.

Fred Emanuels

In times of heavy harvest the Coast Miwok would probably have more than one such acorn granary near his lodge. The acorns from the tan oaks were cooked, then eaten as mush, soup, or bread. Prone to gamble, the native often risked his excess acorn supply on the outcome of a game of chance. The granary above has been built at Kule Loklo, the Miwok village reconstructed at Point Reyes National Seashore, Olema.

Fred Emanuels

A sleeping shelter used on hot days or nights at Kule Loklo, Point Reyes National Seashore.

Fred Emanuels

A partially constructed family house with willow frame to be covered with tule bundles or mats at Kule Loklo, a replica of a Coast Miwok village at the Point Reyes National Seashore.

COSTANOAN

The Costanoans inhabited an area outlined by the Pacific Ocean on the west, the Coast Range on the east, and a line drawn from Carmel across the Salinas Valley on the south. Their northerly limits were the Golden Gate, Carquinez Strait, and the Sacramento River approximately as far upstream as Suisun Bay.

Sixteen communities of widespread villages, are known to have made up the principal Costanoan population. Over this 100-mile long area the inhabitants lived under many different conditions and practiced different ways of life.

Scribes traveling with the two earliest explorers, Gaspar de Portolá (1769) and Juan Bautista de Anza (1774), relate how friendly the Indians treated them and how generously they gave food to the expeditions.

Fray Juan Crespi, chaplain and diarist for Portolá's trek, the first into California, wrote a friend in Mexico describing the day-to-day events of the expedition:

> October 24, 1769 [a few miles north of Año Nuevo on the San Mateo County Coast]: "Here we stopped close to a large village of well behaved good heathens, who greeted us with loud cheers and rejoiced greatly at our coming. At this village there was a very large grass-roofed house, round like a half orange which could hold everyone in the village. Around the big house they had many little houses of split sticks set upright..."

Father Crespi first described the village assembly house and secondly the warm dwellings used by Northern California's coastal Indians and those in the high Sierra. The "sticks" were slabs of wood split off trees by the use of stone wedges pounded with wooden mallets. Set upright, leaning in to the center, the slabs shed rain far better than the domed willow-framed, thatched houses used elsewhere. Partly because they covered a smaller area, and partly because

Jose Cardero

Jose Cardero saw this scene of the extensive construction by the Indians under the direction of the padres, in 1791. He labeled his sketch Vista de la Convento, Yglecia y Ranchería de los Mission de Carmelo.

At this time the compound was well on its way to its final form but obviously no work had commenced on what would be the handsome stone church. Beside the Indians and mission fathers, those in the sketch would be visitors and crewmen from the ship commanded by Alejandro Malaspina.

of the two or even three layers of slabs, these conical-shaped huts were the warmest of all. Father Crespi continues:

"These heathens presented us with many black and white-colored tamales; the white tamales were made of acorns, and they said the black ones were very good too. They showed us two or three bags of the wild tobacco they use, and our people took all they wanted. One old heathen came up smoking a very large and well carven (sic) Indian pipe made of hard stone.

"The Indians almost all carry tall red-colored staffs, some with many feathers; they presented four of them to Sergeant Don Francisco Ortega...wearing a sort of wreath made of green leaves on their heads. They all go naked and bare-headed and all of them are well-featured, stout and bearded.

Louis Choris, 1816

Otto von Kotzebue, Russian naval officer and explorer, commanded two voyages around the world. On his first, 1815-17, the artist Louis Choris viewed Central Californian Indians while in port at Monterey. His renditions came to public attention when his book Pictoresque Autour de Monde *was issued in 1822. This is his impression of Mission Dolores Indians in their ceremonial headdresses.*

"October 24-26, 1769 at San Gregorio Creek [about 10 miles north of the last entry]...Here there is a large village with many grass-covered houses. The whole of the big village came over, all of them well-behaved heathens...indeed all men hereabouts go wholly naked...very happy and friendly, bringing a new lot of tamales at every meal-time."

Jose Cardero, 1791

Note the woman drawn by Jose Cardero at Monterey in 1791 is wearing a rabbit skin cape, a straw skirt with a whitish-warm gray over-coverlet. Carrying a basket would be normal for her as would going barefoot. The artist may have taken license when he included her necklace and the apparent buttons and buttonholes in her over-coverlet.

Museo Naval Collection, Madrid. Univ. of California Press

The reception of Count Jean François Galaup La Perouse at Mission San Carlos Borromeo at Carmel in 1786 honored the first foreign visitor to come to California since Francis Drake came in June, 1579. This is also the first picture of California Indians by an artist who saw them. Father Fermin Francisco Lasuen, Serra's successor is standing in the doorway of Mission Carmel's fifth church (1783-1793). Note the three Indians pulling the cords of the Mission bells, to the right of the chapel. One can't help wonder at the first in the line of the Indians: a horse. La Perouse wrote this about the event: "before we entered the church, we crossed a square, where the Indians of both sexes formed a line; but their countenances showed no sign of surprise at our arrival, and even left it doubtful whether we should become the object of their conversation during the remainder of the day."

Two explorers called at the port of Monterey and left accounts of what they saw which were anything but flattering. The Frenchman La Perouse arrived in 1786 and the Spaniard José Espinosa y Tallo anchored there in 1792. The latter wrote:

"The Indians attached to the Mission San Carlos are...dark in color and seem to be the slowest witted, as they are the ugliest and dirtiest of all the natives of America...the result of torpor due to the fact they have not used the facilities they possess...they till the soil, look after stock, build houses and make tools, performing all the ordinary tasks of a carpenter."

This account hardly credits the natives for having lived for a millennium under the same conditions. The Spaniard goes on:

"Men and women go about naked, feeding in the fields like brute beasts or gathering seeds for the winter. Among the habits they still retain it has been noticed in their leisure moments they will lie on the ground face downward for whole hours with the greatest content."

In war, "they always attack suddenly or treacherously, but few are killed in any encounter, since, when two or three have fallen, the rest run away, and they return to their original false friendships.

"The women...show praiseworthy tenderness in their care of their children, for whose sake they undergo the greatest labors and dangers."

Alejandro Malspina recounted virtually the same observations and added:

"In their *rancherías* they make their meals of seafood which the sea has spread upon the beach in unspeakable abundance, thus saving them the work of fishing. They are very skillful hunters. To kill deer they put on the stuffed head of an already killed deer and then stalk close enough to shoot with an arrow and secure their game."

Other writers have pointed out that the Monterey Bay Indians lacked the balsa canoe, intimating they were too lazy to make them. Yet, their fellow Costanoans to the north, all around San Francisco Bay, did make them.

Jose Cardero

This is a view of the Monterey Presidio in 1791, looking toward the harbor. It shows Indians at various tasks and three or four at the left under possible duress.

As for war between the Costanoans, almost continual skirmishes did take place among those in the Salinas Valley and their neighbors over the adjacent hills. They seem to have hated each other but made peace regardless of whether or not they succeeded in taking vengeance.

In the seventeen years after Father Junipero Serra built Mission San Carlos (1770), the missionaries constructed seven more missions in Costanoan territory. Hence few natives, if any, escaped the mission influence.

The daily schedule in the missions was routine. The Indians attended morning service, ate a breakfast of barley mush, and then trooped off to their assigned work in the fields or shops, or at construction or domestic jobs. At midday they ate a gruel of beans, barley, and peas. Following their evening meal of the usual gruel, sometimes containing bits of meat, they attended an evening church service.

Louis Choris, Univ. of California Press

In this view of what became known as the San Francisco Presidio, Louis Choris pictured the Golden Gate and the enclosed Presidio. He also shows three groups of Indians. To the far left a mounted soldier appears to be prodding along three neophytes. To the right lower center another mounted soldier has ten natives he is urging forward. In between is a group of five or six Indians who might be gambling, a favorite occupation when no other duties confronted them.

William Gottlieb Telesius von Tilenau, Univ. of California Press

This view of the San Francisco Presidio and the area in front of it, now Crissy Field, is the work of artist Tilenau who saw this scene in 1806 from the deck of the Russian Ship Juno. This foreign vessel came to S. F. Bay in search of a source of food for the famished Russian colonists in the north. Nikolai Rezenov made arrangements to conduct future trade with the Californians. Six years later when the Russians founded Fort Ross they found the Spanish had changed their minds. They feared the occupation and let the invaders know they wanted no intercourse with them.

There had to be a considerable amount of balsa traffic on San Francisco Bay. Early accounts, before 1785, state about 100 persons lived in a village at the mouth of Wildcat Canyon in the East Bay and there were two more on the same shore, one near Rodeo and the other near Pinole, each with between 400 and 500 people. Another indication of a large number of Indians living on the Bay front is the immense shell mound left at Emeryville.

Costanoan Indians fighting a mounted Spanish soldier. Note the thatched house at right. The women are wearing tule front aprons, buckskin rear aprons and otter skin robes. Pencil drawing is probably by Tomás de Suria who visited Monterey in 1791 on the Spanish exploring vessel commanded by Alejandro Malaspina. One may rightly wonder did Suria actually see such a scene or did he imagine this is the way it could have been enacted? If he actually witnessed this charge by a mounted Spaniard intent on piercing one Indian, surely the survivors would have made quick work of him.

For those Indians who gave up their way of life to join their relatives in the missions, life became intolerable. Those born within the mission system did as they were told, and were unprepared to fend for themselves after the Mexican Government gave away the vast mission lands and the Church freed the converts.

While many Indians slaved for their sustenance, occasionally some natives took part in enlightened activities. At Mission San José, Father Durán, a skilled musician in his own right, wrote some music and during about twelve years he trained approximately two dozen Indians to perform in concert. He guided his neophytes into making their own flutes, trumpets, drums, and even violins. The group performed for Mission celebrations, visiting dignitaries, and feast days.

Jose Cardero

Jose Cardero saw these three Indians at Monterey in 1791. He was the artist who accompanied Alejandro Malaspina on Spain's first exploring expedition to the west coast of North America following his country's establishing the missions here.

He drew the two figures to the right as one would expect on a moderate to warm day. The woman is carrying a "bucket" for collecting and the man his bow and quiver full of arrows, otherwise nude.

The central figure is dressed as though the day was cold, even damp with fog. Her front skirt is made of grass or rushes, her rear skirt of a hide and over all she has on a cape of otter skin. For ornaments she wears a string of shell or beads of bone as a necklace and from her ears more beads.

Men and boys who lived around the more northerly shores of San Francisco Bay wore absolutely no clothing except during cold weather. To insulate themselves from the cold fogs and wind, they would plaster their bodies with mud. If a day were to heat up they simply peeled off the dried dirt. Most of them did own a fur large enough for a shoulder covering which they used on occasions.

Women and girls always wore some kind of clothing, an apron of tule or bulrush in front and another in back which hung from a girdle which they tied around their waists. In cold weather women wore a cape made of either feathers or of strips of otter skin, twisted. They often wore ornaments made from shells and feathers.

Important events, such as the seasons for hunting, fishing, and acorn-gathering were occasions to hold dances. In dancing the Indians kept time by the clapping of hands, blowing on pipes, beating on skin drums, and rattling tortoise shells filled with pebbles.

As to the natives' honesty, it is safe to say they would not steal from one another, all having so little. But from the invaders they would steal any time they thought it safe to do so.

Mission Dolores eventually contained 1,000 converts. Keeping order in a community that size of rough men and women fell to the lot of four or five soldiers and two or three priests. When one considers the native population was being made to live a wholly different course of life than that to which they had been born, there must have been a mild and forbearing treatment given them in spite of the threat of arms in the hands of a few soldiers.

Both priests and converts had as a principal task the raising of food. For the population at Mission Dolores it is said that forty to fifty head of cattle were slaughtered weekly.

The Indians combed wool, spun and weaved it. They butchered cattle for their hides which they stretched and dried and made ready for the trading vessels. They made soap, melted tallow, were employed as cabinet makers, carpenters, and harvested beans, peas and corn.

All the girls and women lived in separate houses, and were

sometimes allowed to go out in the daytime alone, but never at night. As soon as a girl married she was permitted her freedom and went to live with her husband in one of the Indian villages attached to the Mission.

The most toilsome, weary, repetitive task was left to the women, the grinding of corn.

The herds of Mission livestock remained out in the open year round. Only enough horses and oxen as would be needed for daily tasks were kept corralled. Oxen hauled all transport and horses only carried riders.

Lowie Museum, Berkeley, Calif.
This Costanoan Indian at Monterey is carrying his animal skin (bear?) quiver while posing for the artist T. Suria who accompanied Alijandro Malaspina, the Spanish explorer, who reached Monterey in 1791.

Indians were occasionally assigned to work at one of the presidios. Usually their task masters were the soldiers or their officers who took a less enlightened view of the natives' welfare than the mission fathers. They often worked harder and longer hours and listened to verbal abuse from the soldiers guarding them.

Although the natives were never paid for their labors at the missions, when working at the presidios they did receive compensation in the form of used clothing or beads.

Louis Choris, 1816

These Indians at Mission Dolores might gamble all day and night losing down to their last piece of clothing which the loser would hand over to the winner, leaving the game naked, yet he would show no concern and go about his day's duties as if he had won. Natives often gambled away their store of acorns or dried fish leaving their families without a winter's sustenance.

COSTANOAN

Louis Choris

Louis Choris watched the Mission Indians dance what originally were their native rites in front of Mission Dolores near Yerba Buena, where they were allowed to perform them by the padres because it brought joy into their otherwise dull, routine lives.

The Indians were forced to listen to masses in a language they didn't understand and given punishment if they failed to observe the Catholic rites. When not in the chapel they all had jobs given them, the least constructive work, often repetitive and therefore dull.

Instead of the soldiers doing the hard work needed at the Presidio the Mission priests loaned the neophytes out to the military to perform the most arduous tasks.

Note that only the men do the dancing. Their coverings are made of deer, rabbit, and sea otter skins. They have decorated their capes, and headdresses with feathers. The spears were seldom used for war, often in dancing.

Dr. C. M. von Langsdorff, Bancroft Library

These are Costanoan Indians at Mission San Jose in 1806. The artist, Wilhelm Gottlieb Tilesius von Telenau, came to San Francisco Bay on the Russian ship Juno *which also brought Nicolai Rezenov, best known for his betrothal to the maiden Doña Concha Argüello.*

Dr. Langsdorff, publisher of a book about the voyage reported, "Their (the Indians) music consisted of singing and clapping with a stick, which is split at the end. Their heads, ears and necks were well off with a great variety of ornaments but the bodies, except for a covering about the waist, were naked." Red, black and white were the body paint colors.

California Indians danced for many reasons, all having to do with something of importance in their lives: birth of a child, reaching puberty, thanksgiving, war, a deceased, plentiful harvest of fish or acorns, capturing a black bear, or for a woman being consecrated into the priesthood, etc.

INTERIOR MIWOK

The largest group of Indians in California were the Interior Miwok. They built their villages as low as sea level at Carquinez Strait, also on higher ground in the foothills, and in summer as high as the Sierra snow line, thus connecting the Coast Miwok with the Southern Sierra Miwok. On the west they populated the Diablo Valley (Martinez, Walnut Creek and Concord), Sherman Island, and along the eastern bank of the Sacramento River up to its junction with the Consumnes.

On the east they inhabited what is now Sacramento, Amador, and Calaveras Counties.

Their language, while not exactly the same over the length of roughly 150 miles and the width of 100 miles, had remarkable similarities, unusual among California tribes.

It is no accident that so many lived so well on the abundant food supply of the area. Scores of fish-filled streams ran off the mountains while the alluvial soil that washed into the valleys grew grain and nut crops abundantly. Yet the ease with which they gathered their food may have been the reason for the group as a whole being described by the early ethnologists* as the lowest intellectual group of natives in all of California.

Unlike so many tribes up and down California, they didn't make their own bows and arrows. They bought them from their neighbors who had the proper material, cedar, which they lacked.

*Stephen Powers, 1840-1918 and Alfred L. Kroeber, 1876-1960

While Powers described them as being convivial and lively in their daily lives, they spent as little time as possible providing for their future welfare. Their houses were best described as shelters, quickly erected using brush and brushwood. Out of necessity the Interior Miwok did cover the brush with soil in winter. Observers reported they ate almost anything which crept, flew, crawled, or walked, except skunks.

Deer was the most common game they hunted, with elk and pronghorn antelope of lesser importance. Game birds they ate were quail, ducks, and geese. They did make meals of band-tailed pigeons, red-shafted flickers, jays, and woodpeckers.

Salmon were certainly the most important fish in their food supply, but in fresh water streams they caught trout, and in some areas lampreys.

Lowie Museum, Berkeley, Calif.

This Miwok slab hut and the nearby roundhouse were used near Railroad Flat, Calaveras County, ca. 1906.

The women gathered greens in spring, and many wild plants and seeds whenever possible. They also brought roots home after digging them up with a fire hardened stick. They had a plentiful supply of acorns most years, and this abundance led to the Interior Miwok trading with the Washo Indians in Western Nevada. The Washo were also eager to receive soaproot leaves which they prized for use as brushes.

The Miwok went on to trade with the Eastern Mono Indians who wanted shell beads, acorns, squaw berries, elderberries, manzanita berries, baskets, sea shells, and a fungus used in paint.

In turn, the Mono traded with pinenuts, the larvae of the Pandora moth, red and white paint, salt, pumice stone, piñon nuts, buffalo robes, and rabbit skin blankets.

The small family groups or tribelets carried on the trading, not the larger tribal organization. Each tribelet was independent and owed allegiance to no one. About four hundred persons made up the average family group, living in three or four villages. More often than

C. Hart Merriam, Univ. of California Press

This is a view of a Miwok roundhouse in 1903 at Big Creek rancheria, near Groveland in Tuolomne County.

not neighboring tribelets lived on friendly terms. These neighbors were often invited to join in whatever ceremonies a host group planned to observe. Often the rituals would last three or four days and nights.

The Interior Miwok generally practiced an annual four-day mourning ceremony for the dead who had succumbed during the previous twelve months. There were occasional exceptions, but in common practice the chief of the host village would invite two or three non related villages to join in with his people in these observances.

C. A. Walker, Univ. of California Press

This Sacramento Valley Indian is creeping up on the antelope in the traditional manner the natives used when hunting deer as well. With a head of a buck deer worn as a hat, and with his bow and arrows in his left hand, the hunter would crouch on all fours, imitating a grazing animal. Whenever his quarry looked away he would advance as many steps as he thought he could take undetected. In grizzly territory Indians avoided the huge bears wherever possible. Women on berry gathering expedition often stationed pickets ahead and behind them to give the alarm if a grizzly were seen.

To invite neighboring villages he would choose as many runners as he had invitations to send. Each runner carried a cord in which his chief had tied a specific number of knots. Each knot indicated a day preceding a day before the ceremony was to begin. Each morning thereafter the invited chief would untie a knot. Finally, when he untied the last knot, he and his villagers were expected to arrive at the host village.

The host chief's most important duty was that of serving as master of ceremonies. Since a host always received considerable deference from his guests, such gatherings satisfied the man's ego more than any other event in his otherwise dull, routine life.

The number of villages to be invited to such an event was limited by the amount of food available. It was the custom for the young men and the unmarried males to provide as much as they could either by hunting or buying. They sought deer, fowl and sheep. The host men and women baked acorn bread for their guests and kept

"A camp of Northern California Indians" is the title given this sketch which appeared in an 1869 issue of the San Francisco News. Artist unknown.

baskets of acorn mush heated and ready to serve. In order that the meat might cook well in a short time, the men cut it into long strips before laying it on the fire.

The four-day mourning ceremony was held in the community's roundhouse, a structure in which the Indians held most of their ritual and social events.

In almost all kinds of weather, hot or cold, the host tribe kept a fire going in the center of the building, smoke rising and going out a hole left in the roof for that purpose. Most often boys of the village collected and kept the firewood supply adequate for the four days.

Boys collected pine boughs and brought them to the huts of the older people of the tribe. The elders stripped the boughs of the pine needles and spread them around the floor of the roundhouse, providing a pine fragrance which filled the house.

Lowie Museum, Berkeley, Calif.

Hunting and trapping of small game did yield some meat yet the Indian's main diet consisted mostly of plant foods. These quail hair nooses are set in openings prepared for them. In many brushy or chaparral areas Indians regularly set fires to open up the countryside and make hunting easier. Experiments carried out emphasized the Indian's better understanding than ours of this practice.

Before a burn their deer count was 30 per square mile. A year after the burn the count rose to 98, practically three times the number before. The second year after the burn the number of deer counted in the same area rose to 1341 per square mile.

At events such as the mourning ceremony the assemblage met in the evening, forming a circle in which the individuals wailed loudly, beat themselves and tore at their hair. Although the ones being remembered had died many months earlier, the women often cried out, wringing their hands while pleading for their dead child or relative. Sometimes the women interlocked arms, forming a circle and shuffling around for many hours while chanting their death songs.

Between dancing for hours at a time, listening to the chief haranguing them, wailing and crying for the dead and marching around, many of them would fall, exhausted, sleeping where they fell.

While these Miwok disposed of their dead by both burial and cremation, evidence suggests each area adopted its own choice and adhered to a single rite. When burying someone, a string of shell beads was often buried with them. These beads would be strung differently than the shells they used for trading purposes.

Lowie Museum, Berkeley, Calif.
These acorn granaries and the roundhouse are near Railroad Flat, Calaveras County, ca. 1906.

The shells used for money consisted of button-size white shells which they pierced and strung together on three foot lengths of cord.

Cone-shaped Periwinkles shells, when strung together had a value only about one-fifth that of the button size shells. However, when ground into round shapes and strung on a three foot cord, the bright pearly luminescent shell of the abalone were exchanged for up to five times the value of the white button size shells.

The Interior Miwok village chiefs held their titles by reason of heredity, yet in practice they wielded very little authority. At his discretion and probably with some of his elders' assent he set dates for his people's ceremonies. Often the site selected for the gathering would be in a sunny meadow, if the village was too small to have its own dance house. In preparation for such a gathering even in a small village, his people would spread pine needles or straw over the area. Sometimes during the event the guests and their hosts spent up to a week gambling, feasting, or sleeping by day and dancing by night.

Over many hundreds of years these Indians grew in numbers, living peacefully for the most part, taking their sustenance from what their land provided.

Their numbers were never accurately tabulated, but from the number of villages known to have existed before the Spanish explorers came into California, the best estimates number a total of 19,500 Interior Miwok, including the Southern Sierra Miwok, populated the area.

These Indians escaped close contact with the missions until about 1811. Certainly a few individuals and probably several families may have gone to Mission San Jose de Guadalupe out of curiosity, yet the earliest recorded baptisms appear in the records of 1811, fourteen years after the padres established the mission. That year some of the Quenemsia tribelet from Sherman Island, in the San Joaquin Delta, received baptism at Mission San Jose.

From then until the missions were taken out of the hands of the Church by the Mexican Government in 1834, at least 2,100 Interior Miwoks were christened.

Due in great part to the cholera, measles, and other epidemics of the 1830s their numbers dropped to about 4,500 in 1852.

1856 — 3,000
1910 — 670
1930 — 763

Alexander Forbes, 1877

This is a sweathouse or temescal Forbes saw in Central California.

C. H. Merriam, Univ. of California Press
This is the interior of a roundhouse at Ione, Calif.

SOUTHERN SIERRA MIWOK

The Miwok who populated the southern Sierra Nevada consisted of some tribelets (clusters of family groups) who made their homes in the mountains the year round and others who lived in the foothills all winter, travelling to the higher elevations in spring and staying until fall. In addition, these mountain people, at appropriate seasons, occupied the same fishing or hunting camps.

The Sierra Miwok lived in conical huts, built of a few poles set upright in a twelve foot circle with their tops tied together. They covered the outside of the poles with vertical strips of incense cedar, in several layers, leaving an opening for a doorway, on the south side of the hut. A portable door made the dwelling virtually airtight but for the hole left where the poles came together for the smoke to escape from their cooking fire.

Each such lodge, called an o'-chum by the natives, held a family of six with their dogs and all their belongings.

They made their under bedding of skins of either bear, deer, elk, or antelope. They fashioned their above bedding of three- to four-inch strips of skins sewn together with a twine they stripped from a variety of milkweed. For this purpose they used the pelts from rabbits, fox, hare, and wildcat.

In summer they moved out, into a brush covered arbor using their o'-chums for storage.

The Miwok who travelled to the mountains only in spring dwelled in similar brush covered arbors, something they could erect in about three hours.

Before white men came to the southern mountains to stay, in the early 1850s, the men wore only a short hip-skirt made of skin. The women dressed in a skirt which reached from waist to knee, also made of deer skin. They usually slit the bottom edge into a fringe and sometimes decorated the skirt with a variety of ornaments. Young children generally went nude.

At first the Miwok were naturally friendly with the newcomers, but continued contact turned them into distant and uncommunicative people toward strangers.

One newcomer, Galen Clark, who lived among them from 1857

Edward Curtis

This Southern Sierra Miwok fisherman will spear his catch in what was a conveniently located small stream near his dwelling. In times of the main salmon run he will undoubtedly find his way to the Merced River where his catch will be a test of his ability to carry a heavy load back to his hut. He is wearing a deerskin skirt.

110

until 1910, left this comment, "They are trustworthy and their honesty is seldom in question."

Clark also left this record, "During nearly fifty years, a great many thousands of people have visited the Yosemite Valley (his home), with their own camping outfits, and, during the day, and often all night, are on distant trips of observation with no one left in charge of camp, yet there has never to my knowledge been an instance of anything being stolen or molested by the Indians."

The mountain Miwok was a good hunter. Sometimes he stalked game by himself and at other times he joined with his neighbors in surrounding a large area where they would slowly tighten the circle driving the animals together where they could shoot them at close range. They shot obsidian tipped arrows. The stone is native to the east side of the Sierra Nevada where they traded for it with the

Photograph by Boysen, about 1900

One of the Chow-chi-la tribelet of the Southern Sierra Miwok in his full war dance costume.

111

Monos.

They fished with hook and line, a spear, a fish trap, and by poisoning. They fashioned their hooks from bone and made their line from the tough, fibrous, silken bark of the milkweed brush.

They made their spears of small poles pointed with a slender tine of bone. They attached the line near the center of the hook so that when a struggling fish swallowed it the hook turned crosswise. They placed their weir traps in rapids and built wingdams diagonally across the stream until the two ends met. Into this narrow waterway the natives placed their wicker basket traps. They made these of long willow sprouts loosely woven together and closed at the lower pointed end.

Late in summer when the water was low in the streams it was easy for the Indians to poison the fish lying in pools. They would rub the bulbous soaproot on rocks out in the stream. Soon the fish went into a stupor and rose to the surface where the natives scooped them out.

Drawing by Jorgensen, about 1900

The typical Southern Sierra Miwok sweathouse as used by Yosemite hunters before starting out on a hunting expedition. As elsewhere in California, natives perspired in their sweathouses and then rinsed themselves off in a lake or stream to rid themselves of typical human odors, and thereby not giving away their presence to their quarry.

The Southern Sierra Miwok danced when they involved themselves in any serious and solemn occasion such as preparing to go to war or to perform a burial ceremony.

Both men and women danced. The men would execute a shuffling step, occasionally stomping their bare feet on the ground while the women danced sideways in a swaying motion.

A drum beat set the pace and all the dancers kept time in a monotonous chant. Their drum was a plank laid across a hole in the ground, which when pounded with a thick pole created the desired reverberations.

Photograph by Boysen, about 1900
The baby basket is carried on the back, like all Indian burdens, and supported by a band across the forehead.

Photography by Dove, about 1900
Southern Sierra Miwok babies were tied to their baskets to make them straight and to keep them out of mischief.

113

Marriage in this tribe had its unusual practice. Many men took more than one wife. Occasionally a man took three or four women. This happened most usually when a tribal chief or a head-man desired to have permanent friendly relations with his neighbors. In that event he married into that tribe.

Such a thing as beating or whipping one's wife never occurred to a Southern Sierra Miwok. The wife would have considered a whipping a more disgraceful punishment than death.

Photograph by C. H. Merriam, Univ. of California Press

This is an acorn granary, storehouse, in Southern Sierra Miwok territory. The oak bearing season is only a few weeks old. Squirrels, woodpeckers and bears were just a few of the gatherers in addition to the Indians, so gathering a year-round supply demanded diligence and hard work on the part of the Indian women. This size granary would be used by a single family. They made it of interlaced branches and grass. Note the cover to protect the acorns from such invaders as woodpeckers and squirrels.

In the case of sores which wouldn't go away the doctors applied dirt, and in warm weather would excavate a place in the ground and place the patient in it, covering the affected place for hours, day after day. Sometimes wonderful cures were made this way.

In the early days the Indians burned the bodies of their dead. They would make a pile of dry wood and place the body, tightly wrapped in either hide or blankets, on it. They would then pile all the personal effects of the dead one along with any gifts for his or her use in the next world and then set fire to the wood.

After the pile had cooled, the charred bones and ashes were gathered up, a few bones kept out, but the rest buried.

Photograph by Boysen, about 1900

"Old Kalapine" was said to be one of the oldest Indians in the Yosemite Valley when Boysen took this picture. Her short hair was a badge of widowhood.

The bones kept out would be pounded into a fine powder, then mixed with pine pitch, and then plastered on the faces of the nearest female relatives, as a badge of mourning, remaining there until it naturally wore off.

In the early days, some Indians, but not all, had a vague belief that their original ancestors, in the long, long ago, dwelt in a much better and more desirable country than where they lived. They also believed that the spirit of all good Indians would, after they died, go back to that happier, more perfect world. They also believed that the spirits of all bad Indians would have to remain in this world for another lifetime and serve as grizzly bears as punishment for their sins.

The medicine men claimed to have spiritual powers. They not only cured ill patients but were given credit for making well persons ill, even at some distance from the person to be so treated.

All was well until the coming of the Americans in the 1850s. Then their efforts to make sick and to kill were without effect and the medicine men lost the faith of their tribesmen.

The grand object of the doctor had been to make the patient and family believe that his course of treatment would remove the cause of the sickness.

First he would quietly go off by himself as if to meditate and consider the proper course of treatment. In reality he would go off to fill his mouth with bits of wood and stones. After sucking on the painful spot in the patient's body the doctor would begin to spit out blood and a few objects in his mouth.

At this evidence of what ailed the patient the family would join in a chorus of grunts of surprise and the doctor would pretend to be nauseated from his efforts.

The Indian women had great faith in charms made of the pungent roots of some rare mountain plants which they made into strings to wear around their necks to protect them from sickness.

While the Miwok were certainly spiritualists and had a great fear of evil spirits, they had a fairly distinct idea of a deity, who never does them any harm and whose home is in the happy land of their ancestors away off in the west.

Photograph by Boysen, about 1900

Mary, daughter of Captain John, last of the chiefs of the Southern Sierra Miwok in Yosemite Valley.

Drawing by Jorgensen, about 1900

This style of house, made of cedar slabs covered with bark, is more easily heated than any other form of dwelling known. Similar slab huts were made by many tribes of California Indians in foggy or damp areas.

117

Photograph by Boysen, about 1900

This basket maker is weaving a burden basket. The one to the far left is for cooking with hot stones, and a baby basket stands against the tent.

Photography by Fiske, about 1900

As in all Indian tribes the women do most of the work.

YOKUTS

The approximately fifty tribes of Yokuts, each with 300 to 400 persons, were identified as the Mariposa Family by the noted ethnologist, John W. Powell (1834-1902). Though Mariposa identifies a county in Central California, Yokuts lived as far north as where the San Joaquin River empties into the Sacramento and as far south as the foot of the Tehachapi Mountains, about twenty miles below Bakersfield.

The Indians who lived on this 250 mile long San Joaquin Valley and in the low eastern foothills spoke diverse languages, often not comprehending each other. They fought but seldom fought to kill. Usually only local disagreements erupted into bloodshed.

It can't be said they had the same or even similar practices everywhere in the valley, so in describing the Yokuts the reader must consider the differences in their dwelling places.

Those groups living in the foothills usually made their huts near a stream while some of those in the center of the valley had their villages along bigger rivers, the Kern, King, Fresno, Merced, Stanislaus, and the San Joaquin. Yet a few other groups lived on the shore of Tulare Lake. This body of water alternated between being so large as to be considered an inland sea in some years and, to almost drying up and disappearing in others. Yet these tribelets adjusted to the conditions and lived there until the whites came and eventually forced them onto a reservation.

As an example of their similar habits and yet of differences too, consider a method of fishing in Tulare Lake by some Yokuts and in streams tributary to the Kings River in the foothills by others. On the

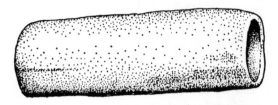

Robert F. Heizer, Univ. of California Press

This is a prehistoric soapstone jar found in the San Joaquin Valley.

lake fishermen built rafts of tule which tended to be a series of smaller bundles lashed together to make a craft 20 to 30 feet long and almost as wide. After erecting a pole frame over the raft and covering it with brush so as to keep out the direct sunlight they would cut a circular hole in the floor of the raft. Fishermen then lay down on the raft peering down into the lake, an upraised bone tipped spear raised for striking. The fish were unable to see the outline of the fisherman because of the raft covering, and were soon prey. A somewhat different version of the same technique was practiced on some streams in the foothills. There the fisherman built himself a small platform over the water, built a brush-roofed awning over it and similarly cut a hole in the floor. The fish unable to see the hunter over him became prey to the spearman.

Seasonally the foothill tribelets came down to Tulare Lake where whole families camped on the lake shore and where an almost unlimited amount of game multiplied. They would erect a brush-covered framework for protection from the sun in the daytime and in the evening they would sit around a campfire, telling their experiences of the day or singing into the evening. They made music with a flute of hollowed out elder and kept time with clapper sticks. One end of a short bow was placed against the teeth while plucking the string, raising and lowering the pitch with their mouths. They used no more than four notes in this music which they used to accompany their singing.

When it was time to sleep, they wore the same clothing they had on all day, a breech cloth.

Louis Choris

These two bowmen seen at Monterey by the artist Louis Choris in 1816, actually had come over the Coast Range from the northern San Joaquin Valley. Their tribelet, Tcholovon, were among the most northern Yokuts. They may have come to the coast to trade for abalone and clam shells. The artist appears to have used the Golden Gate as his backdrop with the men standing near the edge of the Palace of Fine Arts parking lot. China Beach would be just over the first hill to the right.

Women easily harvested clams in Tulare Lake. They would walk, 15 or 20 abreast, in the lake feeling for the bivalves with their feet.

Acorns were plentiful for most of the valley Indians, but they also gathered seeds. These were collected by the women, beating the heads of the stalks toward a wide mouth basket. They stored a supply of seeds much as other tribes did acorns.

Most large game such as deer, antelope, and even elk were killed with arrows at a range of no more than fifty feet. Hunters hid in ambush along game trails and in camouflaged huts near a lake or water course. The elk they shot came after following the animal for several days.

The antelope had a fatal instinct, curiosity. The Yokuts sometimes set up a long pole with a banner on the tip inside a brush pile with a single entrance to it. Bowmen hidden in the border of the brush pile easily hit their quarry when the antelope's curiosity got the better of him.

Men brought in hundreds of ground squirrels by stuffing their holes with dry grass to which they set afire after filling in other holes with dirt. They would dig up the holes they had filled to find several dead squirrels which had tried to escape from the smoke.

Up and down the San Joaquin Valley deer were shot within arrow range by the usual means in California's open country. The hunter tied a set of deer antlers or a stuffed deer head to his own head and slowly crept on all fours toward his intended victim. As the deer turned to forage the hunter would take a few steps forward, stop when the animal raised his head to look at him. Repeating this process patiently would often bring him close enough to hit the deer in a vital spot.

Quail were stopped by a fence to which a number of hunters had driven them. A few holes in the fence which were meant to look like escape routes to the quail actually hid either traps or snares.

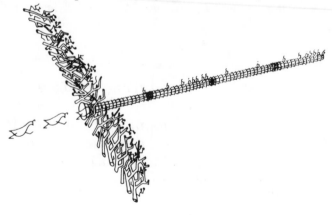

Rabbits were so numerous in many parts of the San Joaquin Valley that they were caught in drives. The Yokuts made nets of flax-like twisted milkweed strings. Often nets thirty feet long were hung between bushes and two lines of men formed human wings at either end of the net. When they marched inward at both ends closing in, hunters with clubs hit those trying to escape and others leaned over the four foot high net and clubbed those caught there.

Each Yokuts village had a captain who reported to a central chief. His principal duty was to insure his people had an adequate food supply. The captains kept the chief informed as to his group's health and as to any danger he perceived from any source. Both

Edward Curtis, 1924

The Yokuts generally snared quail using loops of cord set in a pathway where the birds would see a way through some brush. To catch pigeons they set up brush blinds. In front of a blind they would tie a captured pigeon to decoy others. The hunter concealed behind the blind would capture the birds with a sinew noose on the end of a short pole.

captains and the chief held their titles by heredity.

Yokuts women gambled in a unique way. They were dice throwers and used dice made of half an acorn or walnut shell. They filled it in with pitch and pounded pulverized charcoal, and then inlaid bits of broken abalone shell in it. Four played at a time. They threw 8 dice, counting those which lodged flat surface up. After each throw the women made an exclamation. What, if anything, they won or lost in these games has not been recorded, but the Yokuts did have shell money. A string of it reaching from the tip of the middle finger to the elbow became valued, in the measure of United States coin, at 25 cents. A section of bone, usually a bird leg bone strung with the shells, had a value of 12 1/2 cents.

Mountain tribes, not the Yokuts, made the better bows. As a result the Yokuts bought theirs from their neighbors. They were made of cedar which, although it dries too thoroughly if not treated, is made quite flexible when "oiled" which the makers did with deer marrow. They treated them this way every day during their manufacture. These bows were made about five feet long. The bow strings were of sinew. While the Yokuts did make some of their arrows, their prized ones came from the mountains. Obsidian tips for war arrows also came from their neighbors to the east. They made their own hard-wood tips for the arrows they shot at small game. Some Yokuts shot birds using four crossed sticks near the tip of their arrows. If the tip missed sometimes one of the crossed sticks stunned the bird.

Hunters who valued their bows kept them in a case fashioned from a mountain lion's tail. Valued arrows were sheathed in a quiver of fox skin with the arrow heads pointed down.

The rain-maker, thought of as a wizard, was considered to have supernatural powers. He had a powerful influence over members of his tribe. They accepted him as a physician able to cure them of all their ailments. When they failed to make a cure they were criticized and in more than an occasional failure were put to death on the order of tribal elders.

The shamans conducted a ceremony which maintained the belief that they could keep their people safe from the effects of a rattlesnake bite. Each spring they would make an enclosure of green boughs from 50 to 60 feet in diameter. At the ceremony the natives assembled inside the circle and watched the shamans dance around the outside. They dressed as gaudily as they could, complete with elaborate headdresses and painted faces. They would chase each other, singing and howling while swinging live rattlesnakes around their heads. They let the snakes bite their hands which had no effect on them since they had plucked the fangs from the snakes beforehand.

H. R. Schoolcraft, *Indian Tribes of the United States*, 1865

This Valley Indian is making a basket. The most common materials used were Redbud, Sedges, Common tule, California hazel, and willow. Actually about 78 different materials went into basket making, considering the variety found from one border to the other.

As a result the natives believed in their powers and paid the shamans for a promise of one year's immunity from rattlesnake bites.

Yokuts women wore aprons of various materials according to what was available in their area. They usually wore two skirts of woven rabbit skin, grass or bark. The one behind was cut narrower than the one in front. They wore their hair in two bunches, not braided.

Yokuts basket makers produced a great variety of baskets. In the hill country south of the San Joaquin River to the Kern River there was a distinctive style. They made their foundations of grass coil and the body of cadmium root with red and black bold designs. Each family group had its own favorite design.

These San Joaquin Valley Indians did not have any direct contact with the missions along the coast, though they did have some

H. R. Schoolcraft, *Indian Tribes of the United States*, 1865

In the manner traditional among the California Indians who gathered grass seeds, these women are beating the heads of the grass directly into their bearing basket. Note the shapes of the two beaters.

indirect communications. In the early mission days some of the Chumash Indians who ran away from their missions sought refuge with the Yokuts in the southern Valley. Spanish soldiers who pursued them caught those they could and shot some who they could not return to Santa Barbara. The same was true of deserters from Mission San José.

In aboriginal times Yokuts traded with natives from over the Coast Range at a meeting grounds on the west side of the Central Valley.

After the Americans came, those who took up ranching suffered raids by Yokuts. They sometimes swooped down on farms in both Santa Barbara and Los Angeles Counties. They raided to steal

Stephen Powers, 1877. Univ. of California Press

Because tule grew profusely in their territory along the small creeks, streams and rivers, many of the Yokuts made their lodges of woven tule. Often they built their villages in street-like order. Inside the dwellings they scraped the ground under their sleeping mats so that their heads rested higher than their feet.

horses and cattle, and sometimes they were caught and hung. One rancher, Henry Dalton, lost 1,000 head of cattle in 1850.

So many Yokuts lived at the time of the 1852 California census that in Tulare County alone, (it included Kings County then) the tabulations showed 8,400 adults and 4,613 more under the age of 21. Only 174 whites lived in the County at that time.

That 13,000 Yokuts could have been living in just one county in 1852, yet fewer than 1,000 were still alive in 1910 seems incredible. Yet no less an authority than the eminent ethnologist Alfred L. Kroeber provides such a conclusion in the *Handbook of Indians of California*.

Kroeber comments on the early reservations in which Yokuts were herded as early as 1852. "The first reservations established by the Federal officers in California were little else than bull pens. They were founded on the principle, not of attempting to do something for the natives, but of getting him out of the white man's way as cheaply and hurriedly as possible."

Robert F. Heizer, Univ. of California Press
A prehistoric soapstone pipe found in the Sacramento Valley

CHUMASH

Of all the Indians living along the California coast only the Chumash tribe may correctly be called seafarers. They built their canoes of planks, whereas all but one other tribe of California Indians made theirs by tying together bundles of tule, the hollow bullrush stems which grow in marshes. They occupied the ocean front from Malibu Canyon north to Point Conception and Estero Bay, and inhabited all of the watershed of the Sierra Madre Range.

Thousands of the Chumash also lived on the three most northerly of the Santa Barbara Islands: San Miguel, Santa Rosa, and Santa Cruz.

To reach their offshore relatives they needed to navigate thirty miles of open sea. They constructed their vessels of planks sewn together and made watertight by caulking the seams with tar or pitch. They propelled their boats swiftly with double-blade paddles.

Father Pedro Font, the spiritual leader of Juan Bautista de Anza's San Francisco Colony, in his diary written in 1775 observed carpenters making canoes at a place which later became known as "Carpintería". He wrote:

"They are very carefully made of several planks which they work with no other tools than their shells and flints. They join them at the seams by sewing them with very strong thread which they have, and fit the joints with pitch, by which they are made very seaworthy, strong and secure.

"Some...are decorated with little shells and are

painted red with hematite (iron ore).

"I measured one and found it to be thirty-six palms long and somewhat more than three palms high…when they navigate to fish, according to what I saw, ordinarily not more than two Indians ride in each end."

Only the Chumash of all the California Indians built plank canoes. Elsewhere balsa canoes made of tule reeds were the most popular. In northeast California the Yurok made dugouts.

Actually the Chumash built them long enough to hold about fifteen men, approximately twenty-four feet. They used these longer ones for transport to and from and between the islands.

Anza left this account of what he saw: "In each village they have fifteen to twenty canoes in use and in each one they were making not less than seven to ten new ones."

Authorities estimate as many as 17,000 Chumash lived in their area.

They built their homes in the shape of an overturned half grapefruit. The natives thatched their dwellings two to three inches thick with surf grass.

They cooked their food inside their houses and the smoke escaped through a hole in the center of the roof. The average house was about eighteen feet in diameter. For a front door frame they used whale ribs placed to form an arch. The door was a mat which swung inward.

They made their beds on elevated frames, the children sleeping underneath. They had vertical divisions between them for privacy. Seldom did fewer than four families live in one house. More often than not about fifty persons resided in each dwelling.

Before the missionaries arrived in the 1770s, men lived completely naked and the women wore only a short skirt tied around their waists. After the missions were established the men wore a large cloak made of fur: sea otter, hare or fox. Then the women wore skirts of hide which did not extend below the knee.

Chumash villages often numbered 500 to 1,000 persons. Each village had a chief whose title was hereditary. He settled all the disputes. Each village had its own hunting and gathering areas and its inhabitants guarded their rights to them and infringements sometimes led to conflict. Only the chief could declare war and only he had the right to own pet eagles and eagle nests.

The second most important man in the village was the shaman or medicine man. Below him in influence were the rain doctor, the rattlesnake doctor, and the bear doctor.

Because the shaman's responsibility was to cure disease he claimed supernatural power. However, a shaman occasionally used trickery and slight of hand in "treating" patients. In those cases he would claim a foreign object in his subject's body caused the patient's illness. After the ill person paid for his treatment the medicine man pretended to remove the object, whatever it was, a feather, a claw of a wild animal, or a wood chip or stone. All the time the shaman pretended to be removing the object, he had one of the same item

The Rock Paintings of the Chumash, Campbell Grant, Univ. of California Press
Based on accounts left by explorers the typical Chumash house was 12 to 18 feet in diameter. Some of them had two or three holes for windows. Their frames were of arched, very strong poles and the walls of woven surf grass, 2 to 3 inches thick. They made a door frame from arched whale ribs. The door was two mats, one swung toward the inside and the second outward. A hole in the roof let the smoke escape.

hidden in the palm of his hand.

Certainly the Chumash wisely used herbs and certain plants in order to maintain good health. Many centuries of warding off maladies taught them which vegetation to turn to.

Courtesy Bruce Miller

Unfinished tule thatched hut showing willow framework. Whale jaw bones were sometimes used to bar the door

When nature's remedies failed them, as eventually they must, the Indians called for their shaman for treatment.

Sometimes the shaman pretended to suck out an infection. He would use his stone ritual pipe, place it over the painful area and appear to suck on it. The illusion he created became very real when he would prick the inside of his cheek and with a small mouthful of water, spit out the "infection".

Collection Musée de l'homme, Paris, Univ. of California Press

*This is a Chumash medicine man or shaman from the east
Santa Ynez Valley. He is wearing a ceremonial dance costume.
His skirt has milkweed strings with eagle down twisted among
the fibers with feathers attached to the lower ends. The entire
costume is identical to that of a Yokuts (San Joaquin Valley)
shaman.*

The Chumash made the shaman's pipe and their own bowls used for food preparation out of steatite, a dense soap stone which they took in trade from the Santa Catalina Indians. They also made fishhooks, thin walled bowls and frying pans out of the stone.

The principal occupation of the men was fishing. They either fished from their plank canoes with fish and line or fished in the surf by casting large baskets containing bait. Sardines were attracted to a bait of ground cactus leaves which when moistened by the salt water became very sweet. The natives also fished with spears, nets, and traps.

Many Chumash were carpenters. They made plates from both oak and alder roots. Of course some made the canoes while others made paddles, bows, arrows, flutes, war clubs, etc. Some natives

Alexander Forbes, 1839. Univ. of California Press

These two Chumash plank canoes are pictured passing the Santa Barbara Presidio. One observer has written that the paddles he measured were six feet long. The 1602 explorer, Sebastian Vizcaino made this diary entry, "...a canoe came out to us with two Indian fishermen who had a great quantity of fish, rowing so swiftly they seemed to fly. They came alongside without saying a word to us and went twice around us with such speed that it seemed impossible."

made an occupation of making strings of beads which had value as money. Since both men and women painted their bodies for the festive occasions, manufacturing paint took the labor of many men. They ground colored stones and clays.

The Chumash food supply included, beside fish and game, other seafood, berries, greens, and animals of any size, except the grizzly bear. They gathered seeds which they parched by shaking them into either a large steatite bowl or a large basket, with hot coals or pebbles. Acorns, as with all California Indians, remained the staple of their diet.

The Chumash Indians hunted sea otter, sea lions and seals. They captured ducks by building an enclosure of tules leaving an

After Bartlett, 1854, Univ. of California Press
The interior of a dome-shaped California Indian hut. Note the seed gathering baskets and the duck decoys. The entire floor was commonly covered with sand.

opening through which they drove the ducks. The hunters followed them in, capturing them by hand.

The women stored some foods to eat during the lean winter months. Seeds, nuts, acorns, dried fish and meat most often met the need for reserve food.

The Chumash women proved to be fine artisans of considerable skill. The tight weave of their baskets and the minuteness of their patterns are evidence of their ability. In this regard they surpassed their neighbors of Southern California.

A. G. Treganza reconstructed this probable view of an early Chumash village along the Santa Barbara coast built just above the high water line.

Seaver Center for Western History Research, Los Angeles Co. Museum of Natural History

Typical lifestyle of a Chumash family.

Diorama by Elizabeth Mason, courtesy The Southwest Museum, Los Angeles

Chumash preparing acorns by pounding in hollows in sandstone rock. The meal is then leached by pouring water over it. Later it is baked for mush or bread.

They made plates, mortars and pestles out of both wood and steatite. This stone is highly heat resistant. It is a material which can be placed directly over fire and it will not crack.

Women went to dances well painted and carried bundles of assorted feathers. Men wore more paint at dances than the women did.

Only two couples took the floor at any one time at these affairs. Two musicians provided the music by playing their flutes. As many spectators as wished increased the noise by shaking their rattles and by singing. They made their rattles of cane, dried and split, of sea shells, turtle shells, and bunches of deer hooves. They made whistles of either bone or cane and they even made music with a plucked string. Very surprisingly the Chumash had no drums, so common an instrument among the natives to the north of them.

As has been mentioned, at least 10,000 Chumash populated the coastal area before the missionaries came to California. One hundred years later, in 1885, only 84 remained. By 1906 only half of them were still alive.

Why? What happened to them?

Undoubtedly most died in the epidemics which repeatedly swept through the native villages after the white man brought small pox, measles, and venereal disease to them.

Another cause was the drastically lower birth rate among the natives. Previous to the founding of the missions the natives mingled freely day and night, propagating as they had for centuries. Following the building of the five missions in Chumash territory, the priests locked up the single women at night in one dormitory and the single men in another.

Another reason was stress. It filled most days of a majority of the mission Indians. To escape the hard work and the occasional floggings, natives often fled over the hills to the San Joaquin Valley. For almost fifty years the missionaries had Mexican soldiers to pursue the deserters. They brought back those they could and shot and killed those too fleet of foot to capture.

Museum of the American Indian,
Heye Foundation

This soapstone bowl has been carved out using harder stone as a tool. The decorative zig-zag pattern was fashioned cutting first a groove and then filling it with tar. Shell beads were then set in. Variations of this handiwork by the Chumash have been found in a number of locations.

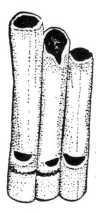

Chumash, by Bruce Miller

The Chumash were fond of music. They made flutes of elder wood or bone, blown from the end, over the edge, whistles of bone and cane, and rattles of split wood, turtle shells and bunches of deer hooves. They made a bullroarer which was a flat board which when swung around swiftly over the head made a low buzz. The marks left by the cord lashings are visible on these bone whistles whose ends were plugged with tar plugs.

(left above)   Flint knife set in shell- and asphaltum-decorated wooden handle, restored. Length, 8 1/2 inches.

(below) This 12-inch long medicine man's pipe is made of a dense soapstone (steatite) using only two tools, a scraper made from a large sea shell and a punch made from a deer or elk antler. The medicine men used them for sucking or blowing disease from an afflicted person.

These are two prehistoric soapstone utensils made by the Chumash: on the left a small-mouthed, thin-walled olla (water bowl) and on the right a comal (frying pan), both from Santa Barbara.

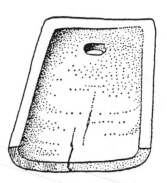

GABRIELEÑO

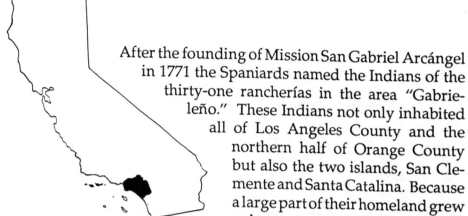

After the founding of Mission San Gabriel Arcángel in 1771 the Spaniards named the Indians of the thirty-one rancherías in the area "Gabrieleño." These Indians not only inhabited all of Los Angeles County and the northern half of Orange County but also the two islands, San Clemente and Santa Catalina. Because a large part of their homeland grew volunteer crops abundantly they may have been the wealthiest California tribe in terms of food.

One authority has written of another unusual feature of Gabrieleño life. A. L. Kroeber judges these Indians as the "...most thoughtful (the capacity to reason?) of all the Shoshoneans (the largest linguistically connected group of natives in the southwest) in the State, and dominated these civilizationally wherever contacts occurred. Their influence spread even to alien people."

Another long-time researcher of the original Californians, Robert Heizer, has called the Gabrieleño "one great family." Where jealousies occasionally were the root of killings among members of the same tribe in other parts of California, these natives almost never carried a disagreement into slayings.

Robbery was unknown among them and murder and incest were equally rare. Whenever they did occur both were punishable by death, shooting the guilty with arrows.

In cases where a single family was attacked by an outsider the Gabrieleño responded as though they were all under siege.

These Indians, after taking prisoners of war, cruelly punished them when putting them to death in the presence of their chiefs.

Marriage among kin was not permitted and yet, in most cases, they were all related by blood or marriage.

Since each chief had the responsibility for the well being of his villagers, and each village had as many as 400 to 500 huts, his word had the effect of law. Chiefs held their title by heredity. On disagreements within his own village he alone made the final decision. In cases where disputes arose between villages the two chiefs made judgement and whenever they could not agree they called in a third chief whose verdict they accepted as final.

No appeal was permitted after a decision was announced. No whipping or punishment was included in the judgement, however fines were imposed on the guilty party or parties. The fines were usually food or skins of animals.

Cases of infidelity among the Gabrieleño were most often settled by the wronged husband giving his wife to the offender, taking the offender's wife for himself.

The chief's authority did not extend over children under the age of puberty. Parents held that responsibility but once reaching that time in their lives the children answered only to the head man.

Although the Gabrieleño way of life was structured, peaceful, and enlightened beyond that of most California tribes, when war with another group of Indians threatened, their preparation took on a fervor comparable to today's military propaganda organizations. The Gabrieleño war dance has been described as a "...grand, solemn and maddening event."

In actual battle the warriors apparently expected the winner would be the best at hand-to-hand fighting. Their favorite weapon has been described as a "34-inch long club of heavy wood, round at one end."

When the Spanish conquistador Juan Rodriguez Cabrillo discovered California in 1542 the Gabrieleño were one of the first groups of natives he met. Cabrillo left word about his reception by the Indians off what we know as Santa Monica Bay. "Indians lighted many fires hoping to attract (us) to come ashore." They swarmed out to his ship in their tule canoes inviting him and his crew to land. Cabrillo didn't accept their invitation and sailed on north only to return after discovering Monterey Bay. He died on his way back and was buried on the Gabrieleño San Miguel Island.

In religion these Indians made it a part of everyday living. Each village had its "church". This place of worship consisted of a circular enclosure delineated by stakes driven into the ground, where to a height of about three feet they wove willow twigs. In this enclosure they gave thanks for victory, asked for vengeance, and commemorated the worth of dead relatives.

Admittance to the church was limited and thus probably valued all the more. Those permitted to enter included chiefs, seers, captains, adult male dancers and boys training for these jobs. On funeral occasions near relatives were admitted. Female singers were also on the special list.

The Gabrieleño believed in a Supreme Being. They were convinced the world was once in chaos until the Divinity gave it its present form, fixing it on the shoulders of seven giants made for this purpose.

They believed animals were formed next, then a man, then a woman, then the Divine went to heaven where he received the Soul of all who died.

The Indians had no bad spirits in their religion, strange as it may seem. Before the coming of the missionaries, they never conceived of Hell or the Devil.

Bureau of American Ethnology, A. L. Kroeber

The Gabrieleño used a curved flat stick to kill rabbits and birds. They made them about 24 to 26 inches long. They were not thrown to return hence may not be defined as boomerangs.

143

One of their understandings concerned the porpoise of which they had a profusion in the coastal waters. They believed the porpoise was an intelligent being created to guard the world from harm. They never killed an owl, a bird they held in reverence. Another belief though not a religious one concerns the crow. They knew the crow warned them whenever a stranger was approaching.

In the Santa Barbara area, and in fact all along the Pacific coast of California, dead whales were occasionally cast up on the shore, and this bounty of the sea was gladly received. Not only were the meat and blubber removed and eaten, but also the large bones of the whale were useful for making implements. No California tribe hunted live whales in the ocean.

Their medicine men were held in reverence. They cured disease and at times created it. They made it rain and of course could fortell its coming. Among the medicine man's cures was steaming a patient and drawing blood, drawn by sucking. How universal blood letting was. Europeans used it too at the same time. One cure used lime as a medicine.

Cowardice was disgraceful so they sometimes practiced enduring pain by lying down on a red ant hill and having someone place handfuls of red ants on their stomachs and around their eyes. They also swallowed large doses of live ants.

The Indians believed mankind originated in the north where a great divinity lived. It was this divine who led the people to their present homes.

As did the Indians who lived to the east and south of them, the Gabrieleño initiated their boys into the tribal society by means of a hallucinogenic ritual. At irregular intervals, decided upon by there being enough boys having passed the age of puberty, they observed the Jimson weed ceremony.

After fasting over a period of six days, the initiates drank a tea made by pouring hot water over crushed Jimson leaves. The narcotic produced visions in the boys. An old man in charge of the ceremony kept the boys from public view, keeping them in a separate hut. They ate no meat or solid food, living only on thin acorn soup.

While under the influence the old man told them about the origin of the world, and preached to them about their future.

In their visions the boys expected to see an animal, one which would be their protector all through life. The animal might be a coyote, a bear, crow or raven, or a rattlesnake.

After experiencing this communal ritual and the boys having acquired a personal guardian, they now had a spiritual nature they had lacked before.

Trials of endurance followed the drinking of the Jimson weed tea. The boys were blistered by fire, whipped with nettles, and laid on ant hills. Any who might fail the experiences were looked upon as weaklings, and probably as losers in war.

Zephyrin Engelhardt, 1915

Scores of Indians are building this mission, any one of the twenty-one, directed by only two priests.

They made adobe bricks and erected the walls, adzed and installed the roof beams, made the roof tiles and covered the roof.

They performed numerous other construction tasks requiring a substantial degree of comprehension. The results they accomplished speak loudly for their willingness and ability.

These adults may have been born at the mission and never experienced the freedom of living a normal tribal life, as did their parents.

In his *Handbook of California Indians* A. L. Krober tells of a myth which includes no hero or heroine but only wicked people and their deeds. He thinks the long life of the tale comes from the pleasure that the teller derived from seeing the looks of astonishment, shock and grief on the faces of his listeners.

"A woman of Muhu-vit, married at Hahamo to a lazy, gluttonous, and stingy man, is said to have been fed with game stuffed with toads and vermin, and given urine to drink by her husband's people. Sick and with her hair fallen out, she returned to her parents, destroying her child on the way. Secretly she was nourished back to health by the old people, until her brother, finding hairs in his bathing pool, discovered her unrecognized presence, and threw her out. Ashamed, she started for the seashore, and threw herself from a cliff.

"Her father threw her his gaming hoop in four directions; when it reached the sea, it rolled in, and he knew his daughter's fate. First, he revenged himself on his own son, whom, in the form of the Kuwot, he carried off and destroyed. Then, taking the shape of an eagle, he allowed himself to be caught by the people of Hahamo; but when they touched him, pestilence spread from him, and killed everyone but an old woman and two children...

"The children grow up and marry; then the woman maltreats the old grandmother, but is killed by her. The husband mourns his wife and follows her spirit to the land of the dead...he brings his partner back, but loses her once more and irrevocably at the last moment."

The Gabrieleño customs and practices began giving way to some of the Christian doctrine soon after the Mission San Gabriel Arcángel started attracting them in 1771. When the first party of Americans to reach Southern California by the southern route arrived, the 1841 Workman-Rowland Party, they found the surviving Gabrieleño scattered and working on the Mexican Land Grants for their subsistence.

LUISEÑO

This tribe occupied the area along the Southern California coast, separating the more southerly Diegueños from the more northerly Gabrieleños. Today the delineation can be described as bounded by the Pacific Ocean on the west, approximately the Elsinore Fault Valley on the east, Aliso Creek on the north, and about Oceanside on the south.

Villagers commonly lived in sheltered canyons or if on sloping ground, near a year-round fresh water supply.

Some small Luiseño villages consisted of only a single family while larger settlements consisted of patrimonially related groups. Villages were located according to the availability of their food supply which included wild game, fish, and acorns and grass seeds. Very seldom did any Luiseños need to walk more than one day's journey to hunt or gather an adequate food supply.

Each Luiseño village owned its own area and remained autonomous from its neighbors. If travel became necessary, trespassing on other village land was forbidden before permission was given. This practice was uniformly understood and observed.

In addition to the customary game, deer and rabbit, the Luiseño caught mice, ground squirrels, and woodrats to supplement their diet. They caught a variety of birds including quail, duck, and dove.

Stones heated in a fire were dropped into a container for boiling. Containers were pottery jars, soapstone bowls, or water-tight baskets.

While the Luiseños made and used pottery containers, which they fired in shallow pits, they also carved wooden shapes for use in food preparation; paddles, tongs for handling hot stones and digging sticks.

Unlike many California peoples, Luiseño men and women shared hunting and gathering opportunities. Active Luiseño women sometimes hunted small game with their men while the old women stayed in the village caring for the children and often teaching them the fundamentals for surviving. Men assisted in gathering acorns instead of leaving this chore to the women.

Men retained the ritual responsibilities and women alone prepared the food eaten during the ceremonials.

The village chiefs held their title by heredity. They maintained responsibility for all religious affairs, warfare powers, and anything which might threaten the village's economic well being.

The Luiseño lived by a number of taboos and observed superstitious practices. In one instance they believed that a fisherman who catches a fish and a hunter who comes home with game, must not partake of his respective catch. They believed if either violated this taboo, neither will catch any more fish or game.

One superstition involved the period soon after the birth of a child. The father must not touch his wife, they believed, until after the child walks. The penalty for violating this belief was that the couple would never be able to conceive another infant.

In addition, after a woman gives birth the husband must not eat meat or any other kind of fat for some days. The penalty for not observing this edict might bring on the child's death.

In common with most California Indians the Luiseño were generous to their relatives but not so inclined to others of their local group. They would willingly lend virtually everything they had, including their wives, and would not expect anything more in return than the thing they had loaned.

One exception to being generous only to their relatives did exist among the Luiseño. For feast celebrations each person contributed a supply of seeds, beads or a deer skin which would be distributed to invited guests from other tribes.

Special attention was paid to boys and girls at puberty. Their education had been started by the old men and women over several years. However, they now received instruction in the initiation rituals into adulthood. They learned about the supernatural powers they were subject to. They were taught which taboos they must observe, to respect and be polite to their elders, to refrain from anger, and they learned the punishment they must expect if they violated any of the rules.

While sand painting was practiced by several Southern California tribes the Luiseño may have been the best at that art. They made them for the initiation rites into adulthood of boys and girls. The paintings often depicted several components of the universe, a spiritual phase of the human personality, or sacred beings, even a night sky with the Milky Way in evidence. When the tribe ended the ritual ceremony all the sand paintings were destroyed. However, Luiseño girls at the conclusion of their puberty rites painted angular and diamond-shaped designs on rocks. Some of them have lasted for almost two centuries.

Diorama by Elizabeth Mason, Santa Barbara Museum of Natural History; photo courtesy
Southwest Museum, Los Angeles

These Luiseño are dancing the Eagle or Whirl Dance. The large feathers whirl wildly during the affair.

149

Each of the earliest explorers, Portolá and Anza, received helpful attention when they came through Luiseño territory in 1769 and 1774. The natives gave the most important thing they had, food, in the form of acorn mush.

It has been estimated fifty villages were occupied in those days. Total population estimates vary from 4,000 to as many as 10,000.

Two missions were built in Luiseño territory, San Juan Capistrano in 1776 and San Luis Rey in 1801-1802. Almost from the start of contact with the whites the Luiseño population started declining. The white man's diseases took their toll especially at the missions where confinement versus the open air way of life they were accustomed to, accelerated contamination.

When the Mexican government secularized the missions in 1834 and the Indians were free to find themselves new homes, some went back to their traditional villages while others went to work for

This Luiseño sweathouse is on the Saboba Reservation in Southern California.

Mexican ranchers. For some of the Indians at Mission San Luis Rey, the Mexican government established several Indian pueblos. These villages did not last very long. Mexican ranchers bought some of the land and with pressure on them the natives abandoned their pueblos.

Changing their lifestyle to become a part of a town with all of its judicial and police practices of the Mexican towns, had no allure for the Luiseños.

Upon the arrival of Anglo-Americans into Southern California, new pressures, backed by a military organization and an often antagonistic United States representative led to the opening of reservations for some, while others drifted away trying to find a place for themselves in the new order, by farming for themselves or for others, still hunting and gathering wherever they could. Today Luiseño people live throughout the mountains between Riverside and San Diego. They are commonly referred to as "Mission Indians".

Diorama by Elizabeth Mason, courtesy The Southwest Museum, Los Angeles
A Luiseño village showing earth-covered dwellings, a sweathouse, and religious enclosure. The sweathouse is partially underground.

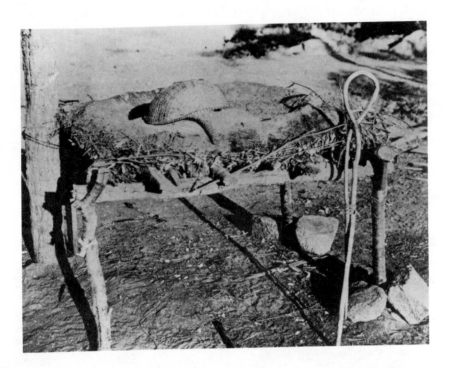

Dept. of Anthropology, Univ. of California, Berkeley

This is a Waksachi platform for leaching acorn meal. A seed beater is on top of the platform and a wood mush (acorn) stirrer used also to lift cooking (heated) stones from boiled food leans against the front right corner. The Waksachi, an independent tribe, made their home east of Fresno, near the present day intersection of State Routes 180 and 245.

DIEGUEÑO

These Southern California Indians were also known by the name "Ipai." They lived in San Diego County with the coast as their western boundary, the Sand Hills of Imperial County on the east and the Luiseño territory on the north. Their southern limits extended in some areas across the Mexican border. While most California natives have been described as having a clear lustrous yellow complexion, the Diegueño had a much darker appearance.

For the most part these more southerly California Indians lived in the hills away from the coast. Many lived in higher valleys, as high as 4,000 feet. Consequently fish were not on their regular diet, and in some places neither were acorns. The arid elevations were not hospitable to oak trees.

California is not a berry country but these Indians ate several varieties in the nature of small fruits. Among them were the wild plum. They crushed the kernel of the pit, leached it and boiled it like acorns. They took more nourishment from the seeds than from the flesh of the fruit. The arid climate made the pulp of many fruits eligible to dry into meal.

Roots grew so sparsely they were of negligible value but flowers were often thick and sappy. They boiled the flowers of the yucca, agave, sumac, and ocatilla either fresh or after drying.

The men went about naked while their women wore what resembled a two-piece petticoat. Their front half was of braided or netted willow bark, and the rear half simply the same bark hanging from a vine-string girdle.

Only in thorny country did the natives wear any foot covering. They made sandals with half inch soles of agave fiber.

Both men and women wore their hair long. The women let theirs hang loose but trimmed the front hair at the eyebrows. The men commonly bunched theirs up in a crown.

Women tattooed themselves by pricking the skin with a cactus thorn and rubbing in charcoal. The most common pattern was two or three vertical stripes on their chins.

The Dieguño had about five principal dances. The more spectacular was their "fire dance." The dancers surrounded a lighted fire when it was dying down leaving mostly hot coals. In a circle they would all approach the fire in unison, stamp the red-hot embers and then fall back. Again, they would rush up once more, stamping. At one instant they sat down, close enough to kick at the coals while shoving dirt ahead with their feet. Their quick motions in unison with embers flying furnished a spectacle in an otherwise darkened scene of action.

The natives' musical instruments were few. They had no drum, unlike most Northern California tribes. They kept time to their dancing and singing with rattles. These they made of gourds or turtle shells and even deer hooves.

The men hunted deer and antelope using the deer-head mask to creep within arrow range of grazing animals. They had no bear in Dieguño country. They killed rabbits with the "killing stick."

After the birth of an infant, both mother and father did minimal work for one month and did not eat meat or salt.

After cutting the umbilical cord they coiled it on the infant's abdomen until it fell off. Then they burned it.

The Dieguño feared the raven. They believed he was a spy and carried messages for the deity.

Following a war in which they were successful, the Dieguño cut the scalps of the fallen. They cut the entire scalp, including the ears, and preserved them. Both men and women would dance in celebration, in their ceremonial enclosure. This area was a woven fence circled area used in warm climates as the dance houses were used in the north.

Lowie Museum, Berkeley, Calif.

In many parts of California the Indians preferred to use bedrock where suitable for their acorn grinding needs rather than use a portable mortar. This granite bedrock may have been convenient for several women to work at the same time, serving the same purpose as a quilting-bee might, making work a little lighter. This one is at Mesa Grande.

When the explorer Portolá and the priest Father Serra arrived at San Diego Bay in 1769, Father Francisco Palou wrote:

"As soon as a place had been prepared and dedicated for the provisional church they (the missionaries) tried to attract to it with gifts and expressions of affection the pagans who came about; but as they could not understand our language they paid no attention to anything but the receiving of gifts and they took everything with eagerness except food, which on no condition would they touch as if it were poison.

DIEGUEÑO

"Intense was their desire for raiment, they going so far as to steal everything of the sort they could lay hands upon...even the sails of the ship were not safe from their hands."

After Father Serra established the mission the military built their presidio nearby.

One chronicler wrote the Diegueño were insolent, arrogant, and thievish.

Just thirty days after Father Serra planted the cross in front of the chapel, throngs of Indians armed with bows and arrows besieged the buildings. All but four soldiers and two priests were absent. While the soldiers fired volleys at the Indians in front of the chapel, the natives behind the building stole whatever they could carry. The two unprotected priests hid in some thickets while the arrows injured the blacksmith and the carpenter. One Spanish muleteer lost his life to an arrow which pierced his throat and several Indians died from gunshots.

The Diegueño resisted the efforts to convert them to Christianity. In an effort to improve relations with them, Serra moved the mission six miles away from the presidio. But for the rest of 1769 no natives came forward to receive baptism. For the first full year only five neophytes were baptized.

Very slowly the Indians came forward for conversion, and the number of hostile natives remained high. During the night preceding the 4th of November, 1775, about one thousand pagans surrounded the mission. They looted the sacristy and storehouse and then set fire to the buildings.

To escape the flames the occupants rushed out into a shower of arrows. The Diegueño killed and mutilated Father Luis Jayme's body, killed the blacksmith and mortally wounded the carpenter. Two soldiers of the guard were disabled.

Nevertheless enough Indians came back to do the work of rebuilding the mission under the priests' direction. The duty to Christianize the natives proceeded and life around San Diego returned to normal.

Pictured are four Ipai (also known as Diegueños), men with feather headdresses and body paint with two women in calico skirts and plaid shawls dressed for a ceremonial dance. The Ipai populated much of San Diego and Imperial Counties, east as far as the Sand Hills.

At the mission the natives learned to manufacture blankets, *ollas* to hold water and keep it cool in summer, and a coco (a sweatcloth for the saddle) made from the maguey fiber. In the vicinity of the mission they gambled, drank, held festivals and wandered from place to place visiting relatives.

Thirty-nine years after the martyr of Father Jayme, in 1814, two priests, Father Sanchez and Father Martin, reported to their superiors, in part, "(the natives) are servants of the soldiery of the neighboring Presidio because they wish to be. But the soldiers have obligations like families to clothe them and feed them, to provide for their education and to give them good example."

Under the mission system, until Mexico secularized the missions in 1834, the Diegueño became masons, carpenters, plasterers, soap makers, tanners, shoemakers, blacksmiths, millers, weavers and spinners, saddlers, shepherds, bakers, cooks, brick makers, carters, cart makers, horticulturists, vaqueros, vintners, and could understand irrigation.

Women learned to be servants and to do needlework.

When the missions closed their doors to the Indians the peaceful and productive years the natives enjoyed came to an end. Dissatisfaction did arise at either going back to their traditional way of life or working for Mexicans. However the Diegueño made a peaceful transition to both ways of living.

As time went on the Indians became a majority of the laborers and mechanics in San Diego County. The men received $8 to $10 a month in pay. Nearly all of them spoke Spanish and some even learned to read and write that language.

In the twenty years following secularization differences between the Luiseño and the Diegueño were difficult to see. Each had villages in which a small number (20) lived and in others as many as 100 lived together. In 1852 some 5,000 or more natives lived in villages between the coast and as far as 70 miles inland. In addition ranchers employed hundreds if not thousands more of the natives.

Zephyrin Engelhardt

The first cart holds Mexican women, wives and daughters of the ranchers. The second contains their Indian servants.

CAHUILLA

The Cahuilla lived in three elevations of principally San Diego, and Riverside Counties and to a lesser degree in Imperial and San Bernardino Counties. They ranged south from the 11,000 foot summit of the San Bernardino Mountains down to the San Gorgonio Pass and to the proximity of Palm Springs. The desert clans occupied the Coachella Valley and populated the Anza Borrego Desert.

Each clan survived by adapting itself to the three environments. The wide range in temperatures and in rainfall dictated the choice of foods available. The sand storms of the desert and the wind patterns of the various valleys and hilltops held a constant pressure on every tribelet.

While mountain springs fed by a consistent snow pack ran dependably, the Cahuilla had to adjust to the many stream and lake levels which often changed from year to year, totally subject to the weather. Where a village might be on a lake shore one spring, a storm might wash it into oblivion the next year.

As streams and springs most often ran in canyons, the desert clans seldom had their villages in open country. Since they were always dependent on a water supply, the villagers built their dwellings around a spring rather than in a uniform pattern of streets. The number of families making up a village was dictated entirely by the amount of water available.

In several ways the Cahuilla were unique among the California tribes.

159

One difference was the concept of land ownership. The lands in and around a village belonged to the group in all cases as was customary elsewhere. But in areas where a family or a group wished to farm, that acreage could be owned by that family and anyone infringing was a trespasser.

Another difference involved the two staple foods of most Cahuilla, seeds and game. Elsewhere the staples were acorns and fish. They stored seeds much as other Indians stored acorns. There were scattered groves where oaks did grow but they were infrequent. When a family or tribelet did have oaks available within a day's walk the people made camp there at harvest time, deserting their villages for weeks.

In the broad treeless desert, catching deer required keen skills. Whenever they could, the hunters would herd the game up a canyon where they had dug a pit, or placed snares on a trail where the game would be likely to run. Often the natives would run a deer, in relays, until the exhausted quarry could be approached within arrow range. Sometimes they would run the animal past a fellow hunter lying in ambush. Cahuilla country contained mountain lions, jaguars, and grizzly bears. While they did hunt the first two upon occasion they preferred to run the grizzly away from their villages rather than try to kill him.

To bring home small game such as rabbits, they threw the "killing stick."

The Cahuilla made their bows of willow or mesquite and strung them with mescal fiber or sinew.

The Cahuilla generally lived in brush covered rectangular open fronted dwellings from 15 to 20 feet long. Where cold weather required it, they built dome-shaped huts. Villages of numerous families contained a sweathouse and depending on the size of the population, a ceremonial house. The village chief usually had his dwelling alongside the ceremonial house. Granaries, to store seeds, dotted the spaces between the huts. They also used large ollas, the wide-mouthed pottery containers, to store smaller quantities than the granaries held. The olla cover was sealed with pine pitch, which made the olla a hermetically sealed container.

CAHUILLA

This Cahuilla dome-shaped brush house in the desert has a brush fence adjoining it which undoubtedly served as a windbreak. Sand storms are common in their desert area. Several of their villages were said to have had 150 to 300 inhabitants. Their total tribal strength has been estimated to have reached a high of more than 6,000 people.

The Cahuilla baked yucca, agave, and tule-potatoes in their stone lined ovens.

They sun dried fruits, blossoms and buds.

Uniquely, the Cahuilla wore foot covering. They wove sandals of mescal fiber. Then they soaked them in mud to whiten them. They held the sandals in place with either a strip of buckskin or mescal fiber. The only clothing men habitually wore was a loin cloth of hide.

Women clothed themselves in skirts made of either mesquite bark, skin, or tule. As in many California tribes blankets were made of strips of rabbit skin woven together.

Girls received their chin tattoos when they became ten or eleven years of age. At that time an aunt or a female friend would prick holes in their chin with a cactus thorn and rub charcoal over the wound. The older women tutored the girls in the skills they would need as a wife and a mother. They taught them to make baskets, to make rabbit skin blankets and even acquainted them with some of the predicaments they would experience later in life. They taught them some of the responsibilities of motherhood. With so much wisdom coming from the lips of the elderly women it is no wonder the girls held old age with much respect.

Likewise, the older men taught the boys the elements of a successful adulthood. In both cases the boys and the girls came to respect their elders as being storehouses of knowledge. The youngsters habitually showed deference to their seniors.

Rawhide sandal with a double sole. Length 26.5 cm, collected in 1900.

Dept. of Anthropology, Smithsonian

Between members of the Cahuilla integrity and dependability while taken for granted, were considered of prime importance.

With all the knowledge passed along by the elders to the young, and the high degree of integrity among the adults one might expect the natives to consider these practices to be of great importance. Actually they thought sharing, giving and receiving were normal activities. They stressed the importance of reciprocity which in Cahuilla daily life became the code. Indeed, these standards of social ethics the Cahuilla strictly enforced. They exacted swift penalties for violations. The punishment ranged from public ridicule to execution.

Title Insurance & Trust Co., Los Angeles

These two granary baskets were made by the Cahuilla Indians to store mesquite beans at Torres, the Martinez Reservation. Cahuilla territory may be called the basin between the San Bernardino Range and the range extending southward from Mount San Jacinto. They are thus the eastern neighbors of the Gabrieleño. Borrego Springs was their southern border. From below sea level at the Salton Sea they ranged as high as 11,000 feet in the San Bernardino Mountains.

Upon marriage, the groom's family gave presents to the bride's relatives. She came to live with her husband's parents. It was here, under the supervision of her mother-in-law that she put into practice all she had been told and could expect to be corrected when she made mistakes.

Divorce among Cahuilla couples was unusual. Grounds for separation included the wife being sterile or being too lazy to provide a good home for her husband.

While providing food for his family in the arid and less well watered Cahuilla territory required most of a man's time, he no less enjoyed relaxing in competitive games with his neighbors. The most important was a foot race where one man's physical endurance would be measured in public, and the answer to the question, who is the better man, would be obvious to all. Men also competed by testing their skills with the bow and arrows.

Women competed too. They also ran foot races, they juggled, spun tops, and balanced objects.

Both genders made singing an important element of their competitions. Especially when women engaged in a group activity, they sang. Both men and women gambled on the outcome of their competitions.

While the tribe was known for its traders, a few Cahuilla journeyed as far west as Santa Catalina Island to trade with the Gabrieleños. They brought furs, hides, obsidian and salt which they exchanged for steatite, asphaltum, and shell beads.

The Desert Cahuilla were virtually free of any mission influence and yet word did get back to them that those Indians living at the missions had surrendered the virtues of tribal life. They came to look down on them, and since they were allied with the foreigners, considered them enemies.

The Cahuilla were accustomed to going to war with heavy clubs and bows and arrows with poisoned tipped heads. The first trespassers they saw were the leather jacketed musket armed Spaniards and Mexicans who came through their territory with Juan Bautista de Anza in his two "invasions", in 1774 and 1775. From that time on every foreigner in Cahuilla country was an enemy.

In 1845 the Luiseño sided with the Mexican-Californians in their fight with the Americans who came to San Diego from Yuma. Aiding foreigners immediately made the Luiseños an enemy. The two tribes met in battle in 1847 at Aguanga. The Cahuilla overwhelmed their foe in what became known as the "Massacre at Agaunga."

After the Americans established themselves in California much of the Cahuilla land furnished grazing for their cattle. A few natives kept their own herds but more worked as ranch hands for the newcomers.

Before the smallpox epidemic of 1863 the Cahuilla population is thought to have been between 3,000 and 4,000 persons. Two years after the disease hit, fewer than 1,200 remained.

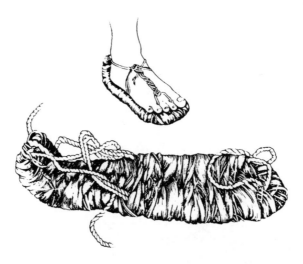

Dept. of Anthropology, Smithsonian

Sandal made of a fiber cord foundation, toe and heel loop, and woven bunches of yucca fibers. Worn only on rough or thorny ground. Extended length 33.0 cm, collected in 1875.

Drawn by H. B. Möllhausen, 1860

These Mohave children are playing the hoop and pole game. The Mohave lived in southeastern California along the bank of the Colorado River. They built these dwellings facing south so as to excape the sometimes fierce north winds. They covered their roofs with a layer of soil to avoid excessive heat, since daytime temperatures often exceed 100 degrees.

The Mohave were one of very few California Indians who farmed. They planted and cultivated maize, one of several varieties of corn.

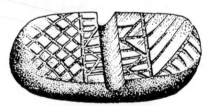

Robert F. Heizer, Univ. of California Press

This is an arrow shaft straightener from San Bernardino County.

Viola M. Roseberry

The Cahuilla basket was used for holding berries. Its pattern represents chain lightning. They commonly used grass for the foundation, splits from sumac, and red scapes of Juncus.

YAHI (ISHI)

The Yahi, a small tribe which inhabited the brush covered hills on the east side of the Sacramento Valley, once resident of Deer and Mill Creeks, Tehama County, were thought to have been extinct after a group of settlers banded together and on an early morning about 1865 surrounded the last village they knew about, and exterminated every Indian in the village.

In 1911 the last surviving Yahi, Ishi by name, half hiding, approached a house near Oroville.

Police took him into custody, treated him civilly, and declared him to be the last wild Indian in the United States.

The 45- to 50-year old native, demonstrated his skill at flaking flint and making bows.

Ishi was brought to San Francisco where he lived under the protection of the University of California until his death in 1916.

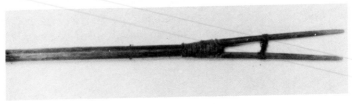

Lowie Museum, Berkeley, Calif.
Ishi's salmon spear.

168

Lowie Museum, Berkeley, Calif.
Ishi demonstrates his position when firing an arrow.

Lowie Museum, Berkeley, Calif.
Ishi shows how to light fire with a drill.

BIBLIOGRAPHY

Brown, Alan K., *Gaspar de Portola*, F. Bonew Companys, Lerida, 1983.

Brown, Vinson, *The Native Americans of the Pacific Coast*, Naturgraph Publishcers, Inc. Happy Camp, California.

Brown, Vinson and Douglas Andrews, *The Pomo Indians of California*, Naturgraph Publishers, Inc. Happy Camp, California.

Cutter, Donald C., *Malaspina in California*, John Howell Books, San Francisco, 1960.

Engelhardt, Zephyrn, *Missions and Missionaries of California*, The James H. Barry Co., San Francisco, 1912.

Grant, Campbell, *The Rock Paintings of the Chumash*, University of California Press, Berkeley, 1965

Hansen, Miller, and Peri, *Wild Oats in Eden*, Santa Rosa, California, 1962.

Heizer, Robert F., *A Collection of Ethnographical Articles on the California Indians*, Ballena Press, Ramona, California, 1976.

————, *Elizabethan California*, Ballena Press, Ramona, California, 1974.

————, *The Costanoan Indians*, California History Center, Cupertino, California, 1974.

————, *They were only Diggers*, Ballena Press, Ramona, California, 1974.

————, ed. *Handbook of North American Indians*, Vol. 8, Smithsonian, Washington, D.C., 1978.

————, and Albert H. Elsasser, *The Natural World of the California Indians*, University of California Press, Berkeley, 1980.

———— and M. A. Whipple, *The California Indians*, University of California Press, Berkeley, 1971.

Hodge, F. W., *Handbook of American Indians North of Mexico*, Smithsonian, Washington, D. C., 1907.

Johnson, Paul C., *Pictorial History of California*, Bonanza Books, 1970.

Johnson, Bernice E., *California's Gabrieleños Indians*, Southwest Museum, Los Angeles, 1964.

———, *California's Gabrieleños Indians*, Los Angeles, 1962.

Kroeber, Alfred L., *Handbook of the Indians of California*, Smithsonian, Washington, D. C., 1925.

———, *Yurok Myths and Elements of Culture*, University of California Press, Berkeley, 1976.

Landberg, Leif, *The Chumash Indians of Southern California*, Southwest Museum, Los Angeles, 1965.

Merriam, C. Hart, *Studies of California Indians*, University of California Press, Berkeley, 1955.

Miller, Bruce, *Chumash, A Picture of Their World*, Sand River Press, Los Osos, California, 1988.

Nelson Jr., Byron, *Our Home Forever*, Hupa Tribe, Hoopa, California, 1978.

Powers, Stephen, *Tribes of California*, University of California Press, Berkeley, 1976.

Rambo, F. Ralph, *Lo, the Poor Indian*, Rosicrucian Press, San Jose, California, 1967.

Robertson, John W., *Francis Drake Along the Pacific Coast*, The Grabhorn Press, San Francisco, 1927.

Roseberry, Viola M., *Illustrated History of Indian Baskets...*, Susanville, California, 1915.

Simpson, Richard, *Ooti*, Celestial Arts, Millbrae, California, 1977.

Van Nostrand and Coulter, *California Pictorial*, University of California Press, Berkeley, 1948.